AFCA's
DEFENSIVE FOOTBALL
Drills

Human Kinetics

Library of Congress Cataloging-in-Publication Data

American Football Coaches Association.
    AFCA's defensive football drills / American Football Coaches
    Association.
      p. cm.
    ISBN 0-88011-476-2
    1. Football--Defense. 2. Football--Coaching. 3. Football-
    -Training. I. Title.
    GV951.18.A54 1996
    796.332'2--dc20   96-8061
                                                         CIP

ISBN-10: 0-88011-476-2
ISBN-13: 978-0-88011-476-9

Interior photographs: Page 1, courtesy of University of Arizona; page 33, Gary Anderson/University of Illinois; page 73, Corky Trewin/University of Washington; page 113, courtesy of University of Nebraska.

Developmental Editor: Rodd Whelpley; **Assistant Editor:** Kent Reel; **Editorial Assistant:** Jennifer Hemphill; **Copyeditor:** Bob Replinger; **Proofreader:** Jim Burns; **Graphic Designer:** Robert Reuther; **Layout Artists:** Tara Welsch and Robert Reuther; **Cover Designer:** Jack Davis; **Photographer (cover):** Scott S. Eccker; **Illustrators:** Keith Blomberg and Jennifer Delmotte; **Printer:** Versa Press

Human Kinetics books are available at special discounts for bulk purchase. Special editions or book excerpts can also be created to specification. For details, contact the Special Sales Manager at Human Kinetics.

Printed in the United States of America   15   14   13

Human Kinetics
Web site: www.HumanKinetics.com

United States: Human Kinetics, P.O. Box 5076, Champaign, IL 61825-5076
800-747-4457
e-mail: humank@hkusa.com

Canada: Human Kinetics, 475 Devonshire Road, Unit 100, Windsor, ON N8Y 2L5
800-465-7301 (in Canada only)
e-mail: info@hkcanada.com

Europe: Human Kinetics, 107 Bradford Road, Stanningley
Leeds LS28 6AT, United Kingdom
+44 (0) 113 255 5665
e-mail: hk@hkeurope.com

Australia: Human Kinetics, 57A Price Avenue, Lower Mitcham, South Australia 5062
08 8372 0999
e-mail: info@hkaustralia.com

New Zealand: Human Kinetics, Division of Sports Distributors NZ Ltd.
P.O. Box 300 226 Albany, North Shore City, Auckland
0064 9 448 1207
e-mail: info@humankinetics.co.nz

Contents

Foreword

Scoring points will earn you praise; preventing the oppponent from scoring will earn you wins. Show me a tough defensive player, and I'll show you someone who can play for almost any team in the country. Show me a tough defensive team, and I'll show you a team that can play with any team in the country.

AFCA's Defensive Football Drills is a collection of the very best individual and team defensive drills available in one resource. The American Football Coaches Association is grateful to many of the best high school and college coaches who agreed to share their most effective drills.

As a former coach who placed great importance on the development of defensive players, I can appreciate the value of this book. Divided into four parts, the book is a great reference for coaches.

The AFCA hopes that instructional materials like *AFCA's Defensive Football Drills* are helpful to its members, and to other coaches and players who want to make our sport better than ever. I encourage you to refer to it and use it often.

Grant Teaff
Executive Director, AFCA

Introduction

A defensive drill book in this age of high-powered, high-scoring offense? You bet. Defensive players and coaches need all the help they can get.

Modern-day football favors the offense, particularly a passing offense. Rule changes have made it almost impossible for a good defensive unit to stop an offense that has similar talent, size, skill, and coaching. So defensive coordinators and defensive players have the cards stacked against them. This more-points-is-better approach may make for flashier postgame highlights, but does it make for better football? No way.

Successful coaches and knowledgeable fans know that, over a long season, a tough defense wins championships. Sure, an offense that can control the ball, keep the defense off the field, and put the opponent in bad field position is a great asset. But when the offense gives up the ball, somebody's got to get it back for them! And we all know outstanding defensive teams or players, even if they don't get the publicity of their offensive counterparts. How fitting it is that the defensive unit for the undefeated 1972 Miami Dolphins, perhaps the greatest single-season football team ever, achieved their glory with a unit called the No-Name Defense. Since then, more colorful names and more celebrity have been assigned defensive players and teams. Sack Attack. Junkyard Dawgs. Wrecking Crew. LT. Soul Patrol. Gang Green. Desert Swarm. Prime Time. Steel Curtain. Orange Crush. The names bring to mind images of toughness, teamwork, and athleticism.

In *AFCA's Defensive Football Drills* we present the practice activities and insights of many of the country's best defensive coaches. All these coaches have a successful system, and they know it inside out. But throughout their careers they've picked up ideas from other coaches and used them to improve their own team's and individual players' performance. Good drills are not system-specific. They work if they are taught well and are performed with 100% effort.

Drill Finder

Key to Diagrams

◁	Cone	C / CB	Cornerback
- - - →	Optional running direction	M	Mike LB
- - - -	Passed ball, pitched ball, or snapped ball	W	Will LB
T	Blocking	DB	Defensive back
∧∧∧∧	Shuffle steps, backpedalling, or walking	S	Safety
∿∿∿	Jog	SS	Strong safety
——	Run	FS	Free safety
⬮	Football, QB, or Coach	○	Offensive player
⟩⟨⟩⟨	Tackle or Contact	⬤	Pulling lineman
★	Interception	OL	Offensive lineman
△	Defensive player	⬤	Ball carrier
DL	Defensive lineman	□	Center
E	End	B₁	Blocker 1
LE	Left end	B₂	Blocker 2
T	Tackle	TE	Tight end
LT	Left tackle	R	Receiver
N	Nose guard	IR	Inside receiver
RT	Right tackle	WR	Wide receiver
RE	Right end	QB	Quarterback
B / LB	Linebacker	RB	Running back

PART 1
Defensive Line Drills

Welcome to the trenches, the point of collision between the biggest men on the field. It doesn't get any rougher, meaner, and tougher than here—the stretch of turf along the line of scrimmage spanning from one defensive end to the other: a crucial battle zone within a war.

Offensive linemen have two big advantages over their enemies across the line. One, they know where the next attack will take place. Two, because of recent rule changes, they can do almost anything but tackle and trip the opponent to complete their mission.

To prevent from being put on his backside each snap, a defensive lineman must have his own arsenal of attacks and counterattacks. Size, quickness, and strength are important physical assets. Courage and persistence are just two of the necessary intangibles. But even the most gifted and motivated athlete needs a set of skills to succeed as a defensive lineman.

Offensive linemen quickly spot and destroy an opponent with few weapons in his arsenal. But a noseguard, tackle, or end who can call upon any one of several techniques is almost impossible to block. Guys like Reggie White and Bruce Smith demonstrate both the footwork of a ballet dancer and the body control and positioning of a champion wrestler. They can fight off a block, fill a hole, rush the passer, watch for a counter, tackle a runner, and knock down a pass. All in one set of downs.

Defensive ends tend to be a little leaner and faster than their teammates on the interior line. Ends need good wheels to fulfill important pass rush duties, cover screens and flair passes in the flats, and stop misdirection plays. It's common for today's defensive ends to have as much speed as outside linebackers, yet still possess the strength to fend off the blocks of huge offensive tackles.

At the noseguard or defensive tackle positions, the first and foremost requirement is an ability to hold ground against the run. A good defense starts by being strong up the gut—at its core. If the defense can take away the offense's between-the-tackles running game and force passes, defensive tackles can then look to penetrate on the pass rush and force the QB out of the pocket.

When you see the defensive line played well, you see what an impact the position has on the game. The Steel Curtain. The Sack Attack. The Purple People Eaters. Because each of these units excelled, so did their teams. Many college coaches say that a top defensive lineman is the hardest player to find when they go to recruit because of all that is required. Programs lacking players or good coaching at this position pay the price.

In this part of *AFCA's Defensive Football Drills* we'll let you see how some of the finest defensive coaches work with their fronts. All 14 practice drills can contribute to the development of skills needed to be successful in the d-line.

Defensive Line Drills

Drill		Coach	Program
1	3-on-2	Doug Adkins	Nevada
2	Pen	Chuck Amato	Florida State
3	Hustle	Tim Beck	Pittsburg State (KS)
4	2-Man Sled Workup	Bob Brashier	Iowa
5	3-Yard Tackle	Marc Dove	Minnesota
6	Hoops	Jethro Franklin	Fresno State
7	3-on-1 With Cones	Ron Gardner	Baker University
8	Eagle Rush	Roger Harring	Wisconsin-LaCrosse
9	Circle	Joe Kinnan	Manatee H.S. (FL)
10	Rabbit and Hound	Larry MacDuff	Arizona
11	7-Man Sled	Ray Monica	North Alabama
12	Leverage	Dean Slayton	Texas Tech
13	Hoop	Jim Tanara	Eastern Kentucky
14	Boink	Paul Unruh	Augustana

1   3-on-2

Coach: Doug Adkins
College: University of Nevada
Head Coach: Chris Ault

Purpose: To teach defensive linemen to react and recognize different blocking schemes.

Procedure:

1. Three OL align along the line of scrimmage. Two DL line up on the other side.
2. The coach stands behind the DL to hand signal the blocking scheme and to give the snap count and cadence for the OL.
3. The coach teaches the DL to watch the football and get off on the ball.
4. The DL react and read the offensive blocking schemes on the run.

Key Points:

- At the snap, the DL take a proper gap control step and read the blocking scheme.
- The diagram's blocking scheme is the inside trap play.
  1. As the RT reads the influence block by the OG, he immediately gets vision back to the inside and attacks the trapper using the wrong-shoulder technique.
  2. The LT reads the pulling OG and attacks the back block by the OC.
- This is an excellent drill for recognizing and reacting to different blocking schemes.

3-on-2

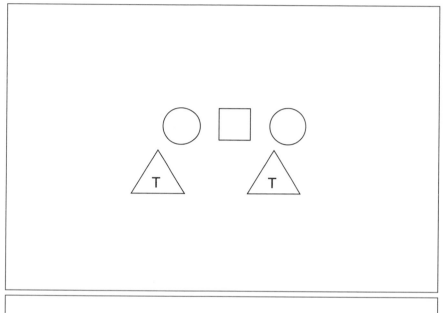

2   **Pen**

Coach: Chuck Amato
College: Florida State University
Head Coach: Bobby Bowden

Purpose: To teach players to bend their knees and to stay low in a good football position while doing agilities.

Procedure:

1. This is a series of agility drills conducted in a pen 20 feet in length and wide enough to accommodate two players at the same time.

2. Two lines of players align facing the pen.
   Sequence of drills:

   a) Taking as many short steps as possible, the players duck walk and exit the pen with a forward roll.

   b) The players face each other, shuffle across the pen, and exit the pen with a seat roll.

   c) The players shuffle over five evenly spaced bags within the pen and exit the pen with a seat roll.

   d) The players start in the middle of the pen and, until pulled out by the coach, execute the wave drill by changing direction three to four times.

Key Points:

- During all agility drills, players should stay low by bending their knees, hips, and ankles.

- Emphasize technique; the players bend the knees, not the waist.

- Teach players to work their feet quickly.

- Use the pen station for other drills in which the player is directed to stay low and in a good football position.

Pen

3 Hustle

Coach: Tim Beck
College: Pittsburg State University (Kansas)
Head Coach: Charles Broyles

Purpose: To coordinate both pass rush techniques and pass pursuit to the football.

Procedure:

1. Five DL line up across from five OL.
   a) Two DEs are outside the shoulder of the OTs.
   b) Two DTs are outside the shoulder of the OGs.
   c) The NG shades the OC on either side.
2. Paint rush lanes so that the DL can practice pass rush techniques.
3. As diagrammed, five receivers are set up at designated points.
4. On QB cadence, one by one DL rush the QB at a depth of seven yards.
5. The DL must stay within his rush lane and put two hands on the QB within four seconds.
6. If the DL has not touched the QB within four seconds, the QB throws a pass to one of the receivers.
7. If the ball is thrown, the DL immediately runs a pass pursuit route to the football.

Key Points:

- The DL reacts to snap count or starts off the ball on OL movement.
- During the pass rush, the DL works on techniques and on staying within the rush lane.
- This is an excellent drill for conditioning DL after the QB throws a pass.
- After the DL has rushed the passer, he will take his turn as an OL.

Hustle

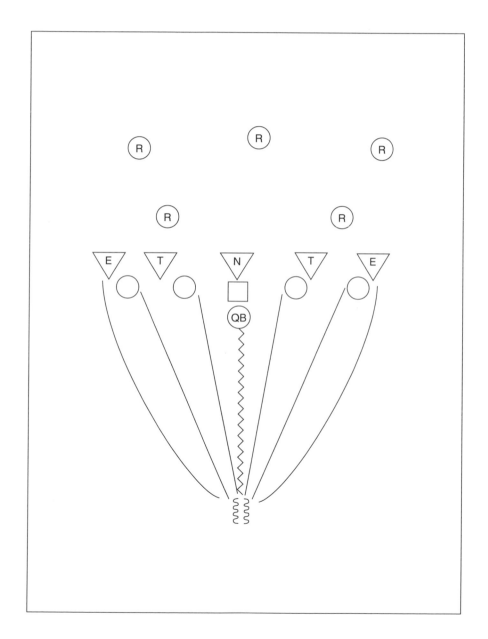

4 2-Man Sled Workup

Coach: Bill Brashier
College: University of Iowa
Head Coach: Hayden Fry

Purpose: To teach the fundamentals of a good football position in attacking a blocker.

Procedure:
1. Two lines of players align in front of each sled pad.
2. Place one cone five yards upfield on each side of the sled.
3. On command the first player in each line attacks his pad.
4. He works to get separation.
5. Once the player establishes separation, he sprints to the cone on that side.
6. Players rotate lines after completing the drill.

Key Points:
- The player aligns in a good football position with his butt down, knees bent, feet shoulder-width apart, and eyes up.
- The use of the sled helps teach technique. The player steps with his inside foot, extends the arms while punching with his hands inside on the bag, and then brings forward his back foot.
- To release outside, the DL uses the "dip-and-rip" technique.
- Emphasize staying low and delivering a good blow with the hands inside.
- Incorporate in the drill the swim- and-spin technique after gaining separation.

2-Man Sled Workup

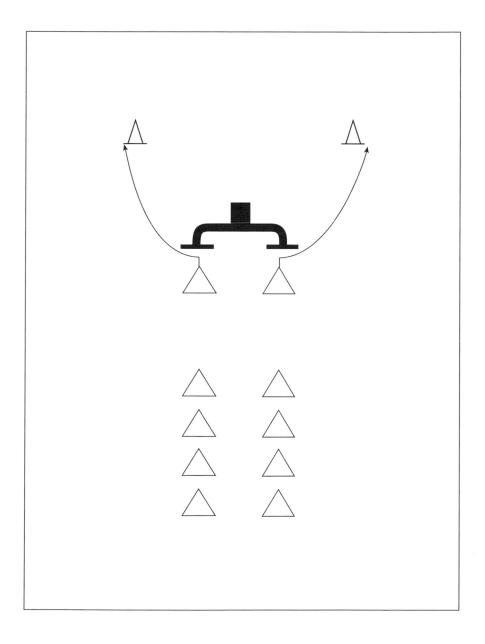

5 3-Yard Tackle

Coach: Marc Dove
College: University of Minnesota
Head Coach: Jim Wacker

Purpose: To be able to run at a target and explode the hips on contact.

Procedure:

1. To teach hip explosion, use a single-pad sled (Gilman).
2. The player aligns three yards from the sled and assumes a good football position.
3. On the command "hit," the player runs straight at the target.
4. The player explodes his arms and hands on contact with the sled.
5. On the next command, the player turns the sled and takes it down to the ground.

Key Points:

- The player must bend his knees to execute the technique.
- The player must keep his feet continually chopping in order to explode his hips through. This drives the sled straight up in the air.
- On contact with the arm, the player must deliver a hand snap with quickness.
- On contact, the player's head is up and his feet are moving.
- Coaches look to see if the players keep their eyes level.

3-Yard Tackle

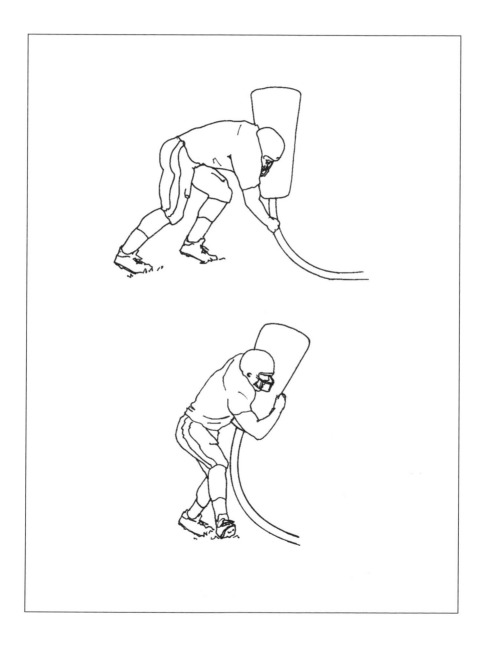

6   Hoops

Coach: Jethro Franklin
College: Fresno State University
Head Coach: Jim Sweeney

Purpose: To simulate a good inside lean and utilize change of direction when rushing the passer.

Procedure:

1. Place three circular hoops one yard apart to form a triangle. These circles are nine feet in diameter and numbered 1, 2, and 3.
2. In front of circle #1, the players form a single line.
3. The first player aligns in a three-point rush stance. He begins the drill on ball movement.
4. The player runs outside circle #1, changes direction, and runs to the inside of circle #2.
5. Once the player comes off circle #2, he picks up a visual signal from the coach who is standing inside circle #3.
6. On the coach's directional signal, the player runs full circle around #3.
7. He finishes the drill at a point one yard past the first and second circles.

Key Points:

- One coach controls ball movement to ensure that players get off on the ball.
- During the run, players lean toward the inside of the circle, almost dragging their inside hands on the ground.
- It is important for the players to stay low so they can change direction quickly.
- Approaching circle #3, players must react quickly. This helps teach body balance and quickness.
- The coach in circle #3 determines which direction the players will run.

Hoops

- To finish the drill, the players accelerate past the cones.
- Make hoops from PVC pipes, couplings, and PVC pipe glue.

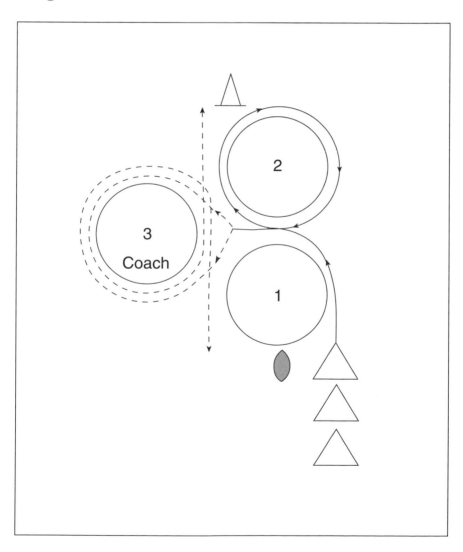

7 3-on-1 With Cones

Coach: Ron Gardner
College: Olathe South High School (Kansas)
Head Coach: Wayne McGinnis

Purpose: To teach the defender to deliver a blow, separate, and take the proper pursuit angle to the ball.

Procedure:

1. The set up has an OC, OGs and a ball carrier in position. Place cones 2 1/2 yards apart to represent the OT and TE. Place a cone three yards deep behind each OG.

2. The coach stands behind the DL and holds blocking scheme cards to show blockers the schemes. He points out the hole where the ball carrier will run.

3. On ball movement, the ball carrier runs around one of the cones to the designated hole.

4. On ball movement, the DL playing the designated technique delivers a blow, sheds the blocker, and tackles the ball carrier in the hole.

5. Drill can be run at full speed or butt off on tackle.

Key Points:

- The coaching checklist includes: stance, alignment, explosion, use of hands, shoulders parallel to the line of scrimmage, and keeping the outside arm and leg free.

- Emphasize separation and taking the correct pursuit angle to the ball carrier.

- Run the base, reach, double, down, scoop, zone, and other blocking schemes.

- Have the DL practice defensive techniques such as slant, loop, gap, etc.

3-on-1 With Cones

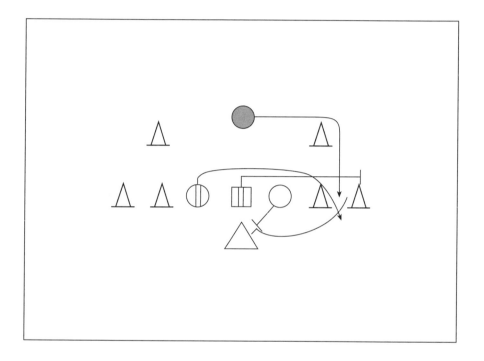

8   Eagle Rush

Coach: Roger Harring
College: University of Wisconsin-LaCrosse
Head Coach: Roger Harring

Purpose: To improve pass rush techniques and pass rush lanes.

Procedure:
1. Five OL and five DL align across from each other (as diagrammed). The DL line up in their respective rush lanes, i.e., head-up, inside, or outside shoulder of the OL.
2. All five DL align in proper stances ready to rush the QB (place a large dummy six yards directly behind the OC).
3. All five OL align in proper stances ready to use blocking techniques to protect the pocket pass.
4. The snap count activates all OL and one designated DL. The offensive line coach gives the snap count. The defensive line coach designates who will rush and which technique he will use.
5. The object of the DL is to get to the dummy (QB) in four seconds.

Key Points:
- The offensive line coach gives the snap count. The defensive line coach designates who will rush and which technique will be used.
- The DL get off on first movement by OL. They must stay in the pass rush lanes as diagrammed.
- When close to the QB, DL get their hands up and stay on the ground.
- The DL tackle the QB chest high.
- The offensive or defensive player who succeeds scores a point for his team.

Eagle Rush

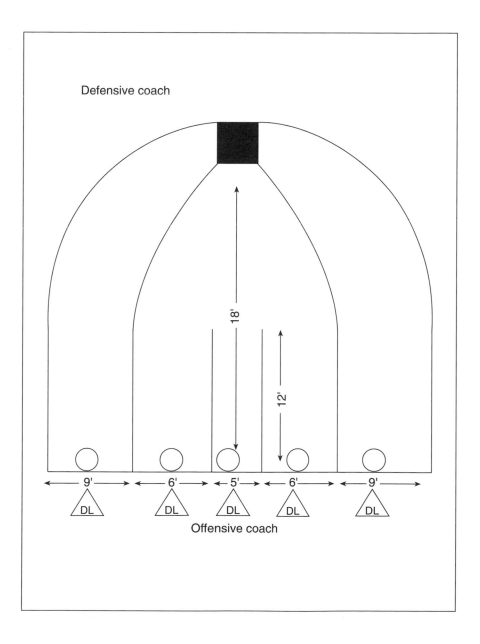

9   Circle

Coach: Joe Kinnan
College: Manatee High School (Florida)
Head Coach: Joe Kinnan

Purpose: To perfect the outside pass rush techniques of defensive ends.

Procedure:

1. Set up a circle five yards in diameter by using four cones or a hose.
2. The defender aligns in a three-point stance on the football, tangent to the circle.
3. The coach (ball) positions himself just inside the circle near a cone.
4. Holding a football, a player (simulating the QB) aligns three yards upfield from the starting point.
5. On ball movement, the defender explodes out of his stance and runs around the circle with his inside shoulder down.
6. After completing 360 degrees of the circle, he continues on a straight line and knocks the ball out of the player's hand.
7. Each defender completes the drill two times, going clockwise and counterclockwise around the circle.
8. The drill is over when the defender knocks the ball out of the QB's hands.

Key Points:

- The coach moves the ball and checks to see that the defender gets off on the ball and explodes out of his stance.
- Teach the defender to run at full speed and as tight to the circle as possible.
- To simulate a rip technique, the defender must lower his inside shoulder.
- By keeping leverage with his outside foot, the defender can prevent the OT from pushing him past the QB.

Circle

 9

10 Rabbit and the Hound

Coach: Larry MacDuff
College: University of Arizona
Head Coach: Dick Tomey

Purpose: To train defensive linemen to make a second effort on passes thrown downfield and to improve reaction to the screen pass.

Procedure:
1. Four defensive linemen align on their backs three yards apart. Their heads are on the line.
2. The coach (QB) with the ball aligns five yards upfield between the two inside defenders.
3. Two target receivers (managers) holding balls align five yards downfield behind the defenders.
4. Upon the command of the coach ("Hip" or "Go"), each defender must quickly get to his feet and rush the dropback or sprintout QB.
5. After the QB challanges the pass rush with his movement, he simulates a throw to one of the targets.
6. Upon the QB's throwing motion, the defender makes a snap turn and sprints at full speed toward the target receiver. The receiver is holding the ball tightly in both hands and extending his arms forward at the height of his knee. Each DL must slap at and touch the ball as he sprints past.

Key Points:
- DEs must maintain their contain responsibilities during the pass rush.
- The coach insists that the defenders run at full speed with a high intensity effort to make contact with the ball. If the coach is not satisfied, the drill is repeated.
- The drill may also be run with one, two, or three defenders instead of four at a time.

Rabbit and the Hound

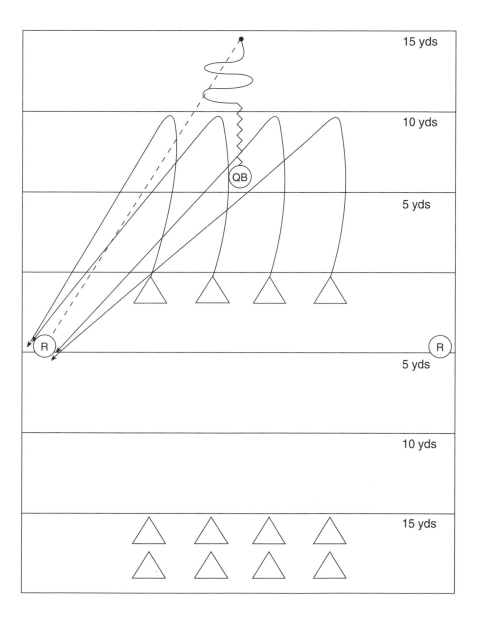

15 yds

10 yds

5 yds

5 yds

10 yds

15 yds

11   7-Man Sled

Coach: Raymond Monica
College: University of North Alabama
Head Coach: Bobby Wallace

Purpose: To develop defensive linemen's hand shiver, flipper, and spinout techniques.

Procedure:

1. Conduct the drill on the seven-man sled.
2. Teach three defensive techniques with the defender working the sled from right to left, followed by left to right.
   a) Hand shiver: The defender starts in a semi-upright football position, chugs his feet, shuffles laterally down the line, and shivers every pad.
   b) Flipper: The defender starts in a three-point stance, steps laterally down the line, and hits every other pad with his shoulder.
   c) Spinout: The defender starts in a three-point stance, steps laterally down the line, and spins after hitting every other pad with his shoulder.

Key Points:

- In executing the hand shiver technique, the defender has his tail down, his head up, and keeps his elbows and wrists locked. Teach him to hit the pad on the rise.
- When using the flipper technique, the defender steps with his right foot to the right and delivers a blow with his right shoulder. Coming from the left, he steps with left foot and delivers a blow with his left shoulder.
- While executing the spinout technique, the defender hits the pad with his right shoulder, spins to his right, and recovers. Coming from the left, he hits with his left shoulder, sprints to the left, and recovers.
- The drill stresses quickness, lateral movement, body balance, and reaction.

7-Man Sled

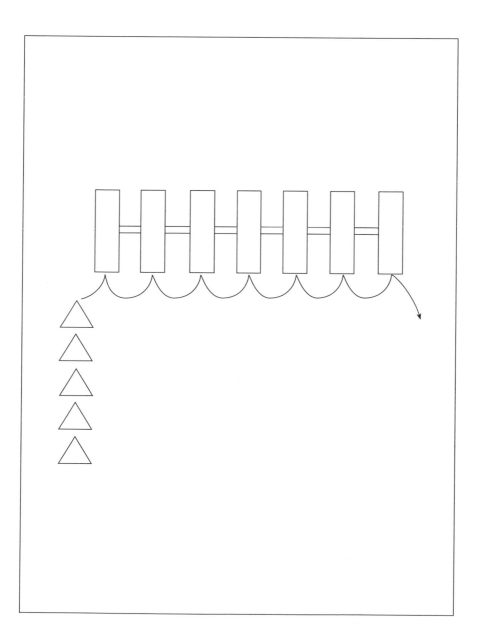

12 Leverage

Coach: Dean Slayton
College: Texas Tech University
Head Coach: Spike Dykes

Purpose: To teach DL proper reactions versus OL's block on control pad (leverage), on free pad (reach), and low/cut block face leg (reach).

Procedure:

1. Teaching leverage:
   a) The DL is shaded, and the OL starts the drill by attacking the tip of the DL's near pad.
   b) The DL attacks and squeezes the OL. He keeps head and eyes in "his" gap of responsibility until a coach signals him to cross the OL's face or release and go upfield in "his" gap of responsibility.
   c) The DL finishes the drill by sprinting upfield five yards.

2. Teaching reach:
   a) The DL is shaded, and the OL starts the drill by attacking across the far pad of the DL.
   b) The DL attacks and works to keep outside the control of the blocker.
   c) When the DL gains outside control, he releases and sprints upfield five yards.

3. Teaching low block:
   a) The DL is shaded. The OL starts the drill by "scramble" blocking on all fours to the far knee of the DL.
   b) The DL attacks, getting hat on hat and his hands on the blocker's shoulders. He releases outside the blocker and sprints upfield five yards.

Key Points:

- All three one-on-one reaction drills teach a low-pad leverage attack.

Leverage

- All drills teach the proper use of feet and hands.
- All drills teach proper release by the DL off the OL's block.
- All drills end with the DL sprinting upfield five yards.
- Work the drills so the DL breaks to the OL's right and then to the OL's left.

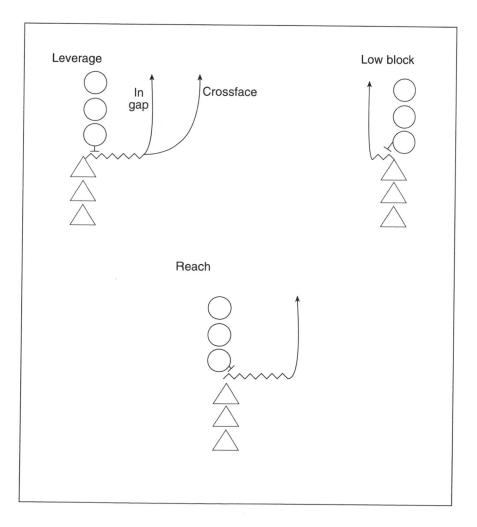

13   Hoop

Coach: Jim Tanara
College: Eastern Kentucky University
Head Coach: Roy Kidd

Purpose: To teach defensive ends and tackles to get off quickly while maintaining proper body control.

Procedure:
1. Place two hoops on the ground one yard apart. Each circle measures seven feet across. Make hoops from hoses or plastic pipe tubing.
2. Right DEs and DTs line up on the right side of the first hoop.
3. Left DEs and DTs line up on the left side of the first hoop.
4. Each side has one coach who aligns himself so that the players can see his feet.
5. To run the hoop course, a player aligns in a three-point stance.
6. On the coach's foot movement, a right-side player starts the drill by running the hoop course. Then a left-side player starts, alternating each time.

Key Points:
- The coach times all players when running the hoop course and calls out the times.
- The coach insists that each player start from a correct three-point stance.
- As players change direction throughout the drill, the coach stresses proper body control.

Hoop

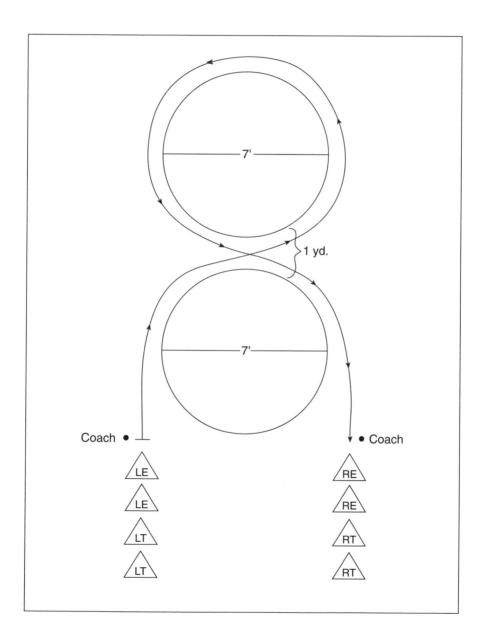

14 Boink

Coach: Paul Unruh
College: Augustana
Head Coach: Tom Schmulbach

Purpose: To transfer the fundamentals of delivering a blow, separating, and shedding from sled drills to live offensive linemen.

Procedure:

1. Two DL align head-to-head across from two OL.
2. The offensive coach faces the OL to signal what direction to block and to give the snap count.
3. The defensive coach faces the DL and signals the type of charge: attack the OL or slant.
4. On the snap count the OL block the DL and the DL execute the slant or the attack.
5. Designate an OL as a ball carrier to run the ball between the linemen or to the right or left of the linemen.
6. The DL attempt to shed and wrap up the ball carrier.

Key Points:

- DL lead with face masks and heads. They should have "flat backs" (meaning their backs should be parallel to the ground) while they attempt to knock their blockers back. Then they should separate and escape.
- Stress the attack—this is "you and me" football. But don't let the DL play around with the blockers. The goal is to shed and get to the ball carrier.
- This is a gap control defensive drill; DL must play with heads up to control two gaps.
- DL must keep feet moving.
- Use drill almost daily during preseason and once a week during the season.
- This is an excellent drill for assessing a DL's talent.

Boink

Defensive coach

3 yd.

Offensive coach

PART 2

Linebacker Drills

Linebackers are the backbone of the defense. They are involved in every play, roaming sideline to sideline. They must have a nose for the football. They should be among the team's leading tacklers. Guys like Dick Butkus, Ray Nitschke, Bobby Bell, Jack Ham, Ted Hendricks, and Junior Seau not only starred at the position, they helped define it.

The term linebacker describes the traditional alignment of players at this position. Outside and inside linebackers typically line up two or three yards behind their teammates on the line. This location offers several advantages, including

- shielding linebackers from offensive linemen's blocks,
- providing better angles to pursue and cut off running plays,
- allowing linebackers to see the whole field and react quickly to misdirection or passing plays, and
- making it possible for linebackers to drop back and cover short and medium pass routes and zones.

With today's multiple defenses and down-and-distance specialization, a linebacker may line up in a three-point stance on the line or out wide covering a flanker. Today's linebackers have the strength of defensive linemen and the quickness of defensive backs, causing nightmares among offensive coordinators.

To defeat a modern-day defense, most offensive coaches know they must find a way to deal successfully with the opponent's linebacking corps. So they send waves of blockers at them on running plays and go to the play-action pass on passing downs to eliminate or freeze linebackers from the point of attack. But a good linebacker is like a good traffic cop. He sticks himself right into the middle of heavy traffic, barks out commands, communicates where people should go, and makes the decisive stop. He is the authority of the defense.

Exactly how many tasks linebackers perform depends on what defense is called. Given the trend toward high-octane offense, backers may rush the passer, go man on a back, or drop into zone coverage. And always they must search out and destroy draws, screens, and reverses.

Watch top-notch linebackers perform and you quickly appreciate the many skills required to play the position. Players do not acquire these skills by chance. Drills like the ones presented in this part of the book are crucial to linebacker development.

Many of the best defensive coaches in the country shared their favorite drills and how to use them. Practice these drills regularly and strengthen the backbone of your defense—linebackers.

Linebacker Drills

Drill		Coach	Program
15	Ricochet	Fred Bleil	New Mexico
16	Box Reaction	Larry Coyer	Iowa State
17	Skate	Bob Fello	Texas Christian
18	Downhill Shuffle	Mel Foels	Maryland
19	Shoulder Blast	Norm Gerber	Syracuse
20	Sprint Tackling	Roger Hinshaw	Rice
21	Piano	Otto Kneidinger	Delaware
22	Slide	Rick Lantz	Virginia
23	Mirror Shuffle	Jim Leavitt	Kansas State
24	Shed Tackle	Joe Novak	Indiana
25	Bing, Bang, Bong	Peter Noyes	Cornell
26	Shuffle to Crossover	Scott Pelluer	Washington
27	Door Tackle	Tim Rose	Minnesota
28	Score Tackling	Jerry Sandusky	Penn State
29	Drag	Jim Southward	Mississippi Delta C.C.
30	Lateral Mirror Tackle	Stephen Spagnuolo	Rutgers
31	Form Tackle	Mike Toop	Pennsylvania
32	3-on-1	Kurt Van Valkenburgh	Hawaii

15   Ricochet

Coach: Fred Bleil
College: University of New Mexico
Head Coach: Dennis Franchione

Purpose: To teach linebackers specific techniques to defeat different blocking schemes.

Procedure:
1. Three blockers align five yards apart on a line.
2. The ball carrier (shield) aligns five yards behind the last blocker.
3. The LB, in the correct stance and starting position, aligns five yards in front of the middle blocker.
4. The coach aligns two yards behind the middle blocker. To start the drill, he gives a flow direction.
5. Upon reading the flow, the LB attacks the first blocker in that direction. He then attacks the middle blocker, defeats the third blocker, and form tackles the ball carrier.

Key Points:
- The three starting blocks are as follows:
  a) down block on the outside shoulder of the LB,
  b) cut block, and
  c) base block.
- Teach the linebacker what every block attempts to accomplish and how to defeat each type.
- The LB should use the rip technique to gain clearance against the base block.
- Throughout the drill, the LB must maintain foot movement while keeping his shoulders squared with constant pad leverage.
- Use a large Gilman playball to simulate the cut block.
- The drill is over when the LB form tackles or tackles the ball carrier.

Ricochet

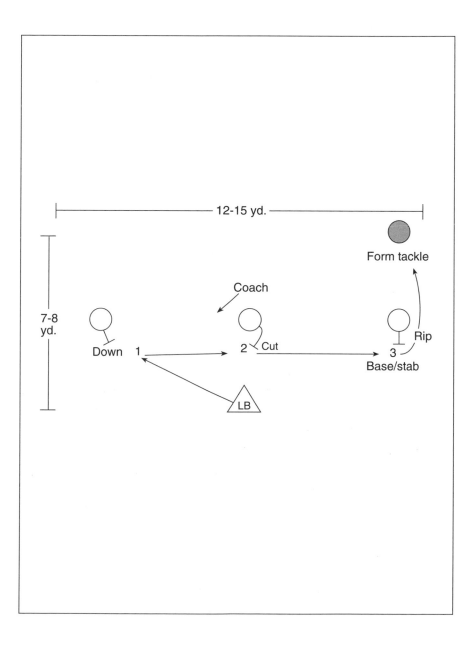

12-15 yd.

7-8 yd.

Form tackle

Coach

Down   1   2 Cut   3
                                    Rip
                              Base/stab

LB

16   Box Reaction

Coach: Larry Coyer
College: Iowa State University
Head Coach: Dan McCarney

Purpose: To teach linebackers how to change direction after a visual stimulus while keeping a fundamental movement base.

Procedure:

1. The drill station is a 10-yard square outlined by traffic cones.
2. Two LBs align one yard apart on the baseline facing the coach.
3. The LBs react to the coach's hand signals.
   a) As the coach points straight back, LBs initiate quick, tight backpedals.
   b) As the coach points at cone in either corner, LBs respond by opening their hips and executing crossover runs.
   c) As the coach points to various corners of the box, LBs react and change direction.
   d) To end the drill, the coach points at himself with his thumb. The LBs plant their feet, change direction, and run full speed past the coach.

Key Points:

- The LBs learn to move and react quickly without losing control of their bodies.
- The LBs must keep their feet up and under or lose their base, slip, and fall.
- Throughout the drill, players always maintain eye contact with the coach.
- The LBs move to a specific point without looking at it.
- In response to changing visual stimuli, LBs respond with quickness and with proper body movement.

Box Reaction

16

- As the LB breaks out of the box, the coach may throw the ball in front of him.
- The LB intercepts the ball at its highest point.
- This drill allows the coach to put two LBs in the box to be competitive.

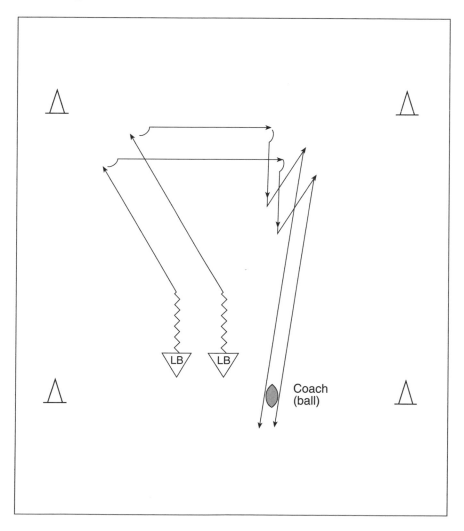

Skate

Coach: Bob Fello
College: Texas Christian University
Head Coach: Pat Sullivan

Purpose: To teach inside and outside linebackers to defeat high or low blocks while keeping tempo on the ball carrier.

Procedure: To drill OLBs (9 technique):

1. The TE and RB take normal alignments as offensive blockers.
2. For drill purposes, the ball carrier aligns as the TB.
3. The OLB aligns outside shade of the TE on the line of scrimmage.
4. On the snap, the TE attempts to reach (hook) block the OLB, who defeats the block with a hand steer.
5. The RB attacks downhill to block the outside leg of the OLB, who defeats the block with a hand shiver.
6. After defeating the two blockers, the OLB executes a good form tackle on the ball carrier and drives him back five yards.

To drill ILBs (50 defense):

1. The ILB shades the OG at a depth of four yards.
2. On the snap, the OG attempts to block the ILB, who defeats the block with a rip technique.
3. Next, the ILB defeats the low block from the RB with a hand shiver.
4. After defeating the two blockers, the ILB executes a good form tackle on the ball carrier and drives him back five yards.

Key Points:

- Throughout the drill, the LB maintains a good hitting position.
- Teach the LBs to defeat low blocks by using their hands.

Skate

17

- It is important for LBs to keep proper leverage and clear their feet.
- The drill can be executed at full speed or can be toned down.
- Coaches praise and encourage blockers to give a good look.

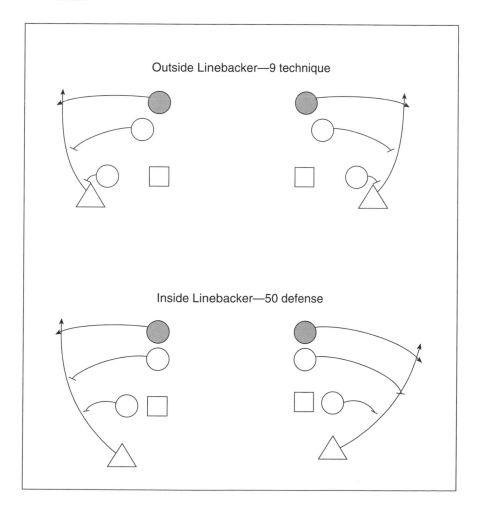

Outside Linebacker—9 technique

Inside Linebacker—50 defense

18 · Downhill Shuffle

Coach: Mel Foels
College: University of Maryland
Head Coach: Mark Duffner

Purpose: To teach linebackers to attack the line of scrimmage, use their hands to shed blocks, and master the angle tackle.

Procedure:
1. Place four bags at an angle within a 10-yard area.
2. Three blockers align between the two outside bags and the two middle bags. A fourth blocker is placed outside bag #4.
3. The ball carrier aligns 10 yards away from bag #4 in a backoff position.
4. Facing the blockers, the LB aligns next to bag #1.
5. On the coach's command, the LB steps with his near foot to shuffle across the bags.
6. Within the bag area, each blocker steps forward to expose his chest when the LB's trail foot hits inside the near bag.
7. During the shuffle, the LB hand shivers each blocker.
8. Blocker #4 will attempt to low block the LB after he has crossed the last bag.
9. After shedding the low block, the LB turns and sprints to execute an angle tackle on the ball carrier.

Key Points:
- The drill starts only after the LB has taken a proper stance (football position).
- Throughout the drill, the LB maintains a good hitting position, keeping his tail tucked under.
- Throughout the drill, the LB uses good footwork by keeping his lead leg up and not behind the bag.
- In defeating the low block, the LB must keep his hands

Downhill Shuffle

down and his knees bent. He may have to kick his feet back to maintain balance.

- All blockers time their blocks with the shuffling LB.
- Before running, the ball carrier waits until the LB engages blocker #4.

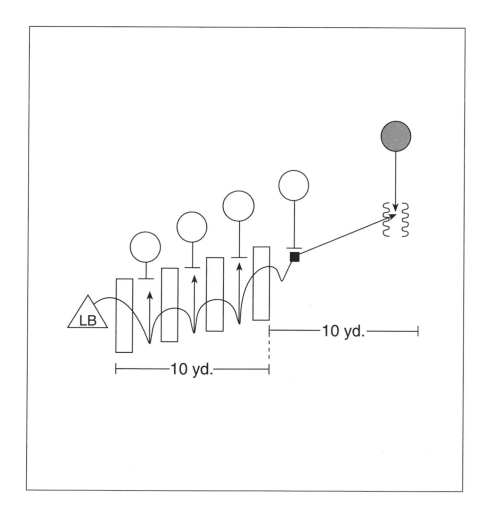

19 Shoulder Blast

Coach: Norm Gerber
College: Syracuse University
Head Coach: Paul Pasquaioni

Purpose: To teach linebackers the skills necessary to fend off blockers while in pursuit of the ball carrier.

Procedure:
1. On a yard line, three blockers align one yard apart.
2. Facing the blockers in a good football position, the LB aligns two yards in front of them.
3. The coach stands behind the LB and signals each blocker when to attack.
4. On blocker movement, the LB attacks and explodes into the blocker using the shoulder blast double hand shiver technique.
5. After exploding into the first two blockers, the LB recovers to the original football position.
6. On the third blocker, the LB, in a lockout position, uses a double hand shiver and drives the blocker back.

Key Points:
- When attacking the blocker, the LB's aiming point is the chest.
- The shoulder blast double hand shiver starts with a power step (inside foot) that splits the crotch of the blocker.
- Upon contact, the LB dives his shoulder and simultaneously fires a double hand shiver into the blocker's numbers.
- When executing the lockout technique, the LB bends his knees and arches his back.
- A ball carrier can be added to the drill. If so, LB sheds the blocker and tackles the ball carrier from the lockout position.

Shoulder Blast

19

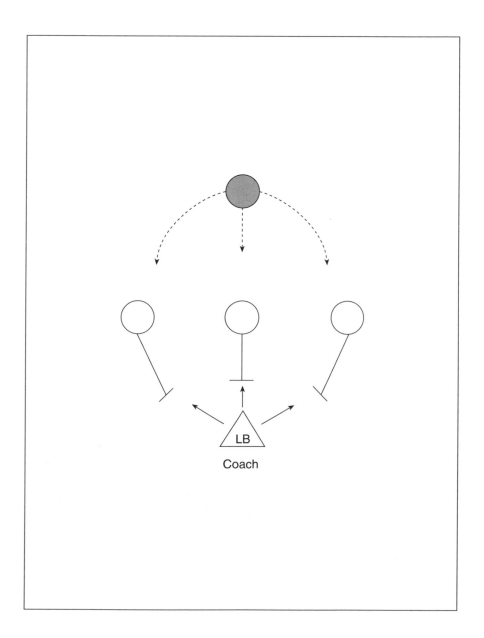

20 Sprint Tackling

Coach: Roger Hinshaw
College: Rice University
Head Coach: Ken Hatfield

Purpose: To practice proper angles and correct body position while open-field tackling.

Procedure:

1. Place five cones 2 yards apart (as diagrammed).
2. Place two agile dummies on the ground to create a running lane that the ball carrier must stay in.
3. The defenders start 10 yards from the cones. On the other side, the ball carriers start 5 yards from the cones.
4. The drill starts with the defender attacking the cones. The ball carrier runs into the cone area breaking right or left.
5. While running at full speed, the defender attacks under control. The defender must execute a proper angle tackle.

Key Points:

- Since the defender is required to cover more ground, he should always be twice as far from the cones as the ball carrier.
- As the defender improves, allow the ball carrier to execute a fake when he enters the cone area.
- Teach the ball carrier to run upfield when coming out of the cones. The ball carrier should not run away from the defender.
- The defender should keep his feet moving and should close toward the ball carrier.
- The defender works inside out on the ball carrier by attacking his hip. He tackles across the front of the ball carrier with his body.
- While turning the ball carrier to his side, the defender must keep his feet moving.

Sprint Tackling

20

- The defender tackles by closing—not by breaking down.
- Emphasize to the defender taking a proper angle to tackle the ball carrier; he should control the ball carrier from the inside out.

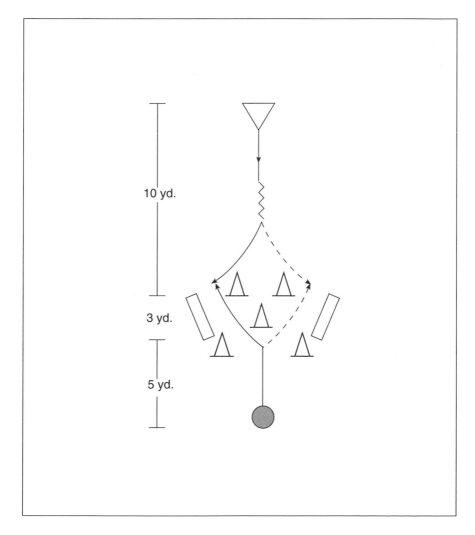

21　　Piano

Coach: Otto Kneidinger
College: University of Delaware
Head Coach: Harold R. "Tubby" Raymond

Purpose: To teach linebackers block protection versus high and low blocks while also maintaining leverage on the ball carrier.

Procedure:

1. Place four marker cones three yards apart (as diagrammed).
2. Two blockers align in the first two alleys of the cones.
3. The ball carrier aligns five yards behind the second blocker.
4. The LB aligns three yards in front of the first blocker.
5. On the snap, blocker #1 fires out and attempts to high block the LB.
6. When the first blocker makes contact with the LB, blocker #2 starts to pull through the third alley and attempts to low block the LB.
7. The LB plays off the high block and then the low block, using proper block protection technique. Next, he executes a form tackle on the ball carrier who is running through the fourth alley.

Key Points:

- The LB is to maintain proper body mechanics, stay low, and explode through the blocker while maintaining vertical and horizontal leverage.
- Teach the LB to keep his shoulders square to the line of scrimmage.
- Proper leverage allows the LB to separate and shed the blocker.
- A variation on the drill is to interchange blocks. For example, use all high or all low blocks.

Piano

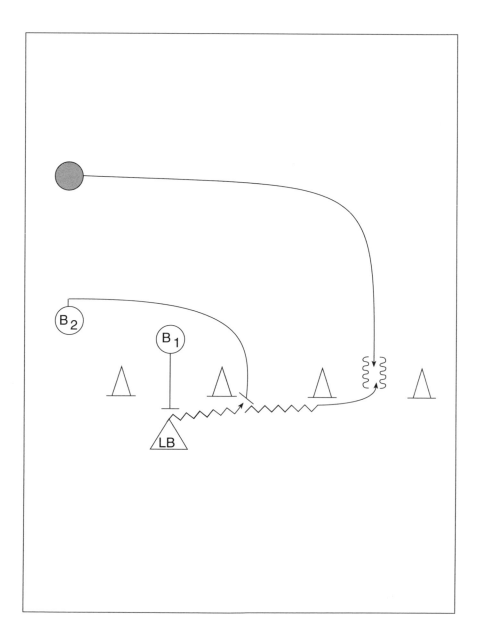

22   Slide

Coach: Rick Lantz
College: University of Virginia
Head Coach: George Welsh

Purpose: To have linebackers learn proper leverage by teaching them how to explode, separate, disengage, and execute a form tackle.

Procedure:
1. The drill station is a five-yard square. Blocker #1 aligns at the near corner, blocker #2 aligns in the middle of square, and the ball carrier aligns at the far corner.
2. The defender positions himself into a correct hitting position (fit) with blocker #1. On command, both the defender and blocker #1 strain into each other.
3. On command, the defender separates from the blocker, disengages, and moves laterally toward closing blocker #2.
4. The second blocker allows the defender to move into a head-up position before blocking him.
5. The defender explodes, separates, and disengages from blocker #2.
6. The defender shuffles to a head-up position and executes a form tackle on the ball carrier.

Key Points:
- The drill teaches proper leverage (hitting position) for all defensive roles and is pertinent to all defensive positions.
- Teach the full arm extension technique so that the defender can separate from blocker #1.
- Disengaging from the blocker allows the defender to shuffle down the line and maintain a proper bend in the knee.
- The defender learns the three-step progression technique:
  a) Explode
  b) Separate
  c) Disengage after the ball carrier is committed

Slide

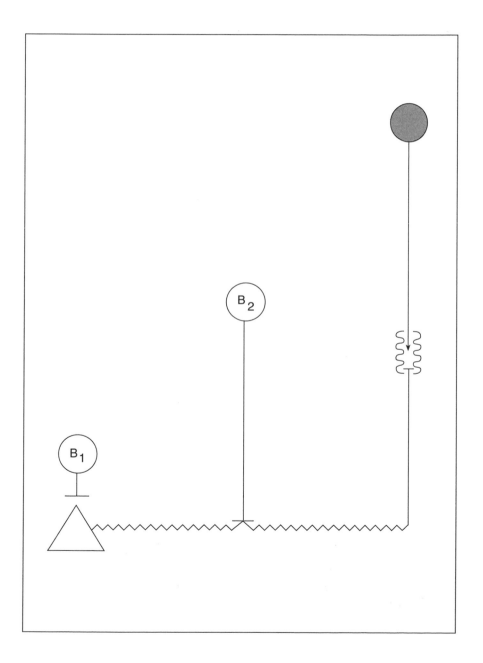

23 **Mirror Shuffle**

Coach: Jim Leavitt
College: Kansas State University
Head Coach: Bill Snyder

Purpose: To teach proper fundamentals and techniques for pursuit of the football.

Procedure:

1. Place five large blocking dummies one yard apart, perpendicular to the line of scrimmage.
2. Position a row of linebackers near the start area.
3. The coach stands in front of the middle dummy.
4. On the coach's command, the first LB starts the drill by shuffling over the bags.
5. The coach moves to his right or left. The LB mirrors the movement of the coach.
6. After the LB has changed directions several times, the coach signals for the LB to exit. The LB shuffles over the bags and out.
7. Continue the drill until all LBs have had enough repetitions.
8. A companion drill involves the LB catching a tossed ball from the coach while shuffling across the bags in one direction.

Key Points:

- This drill is designed to improve reaction, agility, and concentration.
- While shuffling across the bags, the LB must always keep his eyes on the coach.
- Throughout the drill, remind the LB to pick up his feet and avoid hitting any bags.
- Teach LBs to stay low and in a good football position while shuffling.

Mirror Shuffle

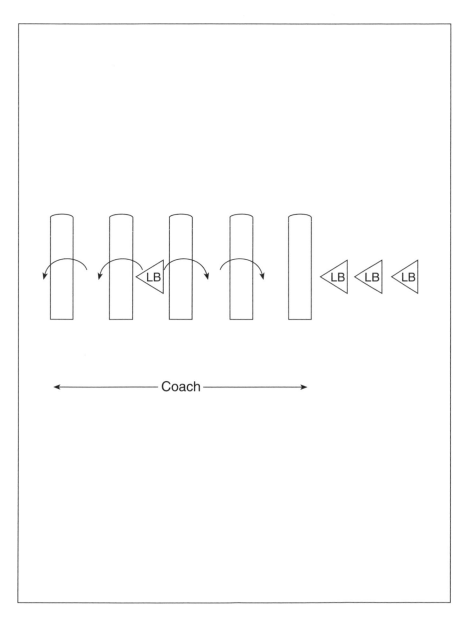

24 Shed Tackle

Coach: Joe Novak
College: Indiana University
Head Coach: Bill Mallory

Purpose: To teach linebackers how to use their hands or forearms to deliver a block, shed a blocker, and execute a tackle.

Procedure:

1. Position the blocker and LB 5 yards apart, with the LB to one side.
2. The ball carrier is 8 to 10 yards behind the blocker.
3. The drill starts when the blocker fires out to block the LB.
4. The LB reacts to the blocker by delivering a forearm blow or hand shiver. He then disengages from the block.
5. The LB locates the ball carrier and executes a form tackle.

Key Points:

- The LB must maintain proper position on the blocker.
- Teach the LB to bend his knees when delivering a forearm blow or hand shiver.
- Proper form tackle technique involves a correct body position, rolling the hips, and maintaining a good knee bend with proper follow through.

Shed Tackle

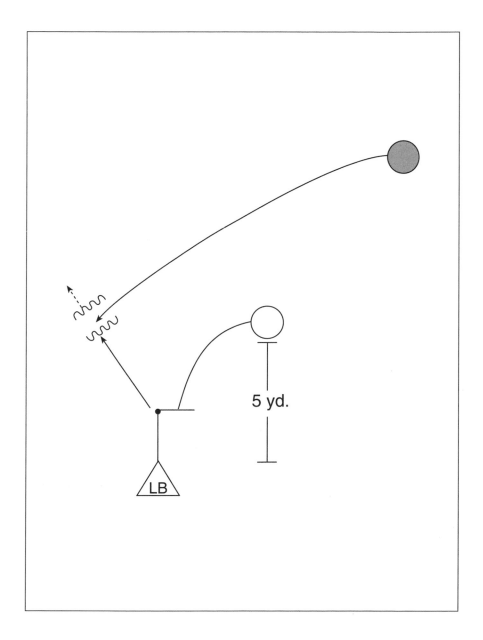

5 yd.

LB

25 Bing, Bang, Bong

Coach: Peter Noyes
College: Cornell University
Head Coach: Jim Hofher

Purpose: To teach pursuit, sideline, and open-field tackling under stressful conditions.

Procedure:

1. Position three ball carriers holding shields 5 yards apart on the sideline. They are each assigned a number (1, 2, or 3).

2. The LB lies down on his back in front of the middle ball carrier at a depth of 15 to 18 yards.

3. The coach designates the order in which each ball carrier will run straight ahead down the line.

4. On the coach's command "hit," the first ball carrier runs straight down the line.

5. Hearing the command, the LB gets up, finds the ball, and executes a chest butt. [Bing.]

6. After the LB executes the chest butt on the first ball carrier, the second ball carrier starts his motion.

7. The LB pursues the second ball carrier running at full sprint. He executes another chest butt. [Bang.]

8. After the second chest butt, the third ball carrier starts running. The LB reacts with a chest butt on the third ball carrier. [Bong.]

9. He finishes the drill by putting the ball carrier on the ground.

Key Points:

- The LB must find all ball carriers and execute a 100 percent chest butt.

  a) The head is up.

  b) The LB makes chest-to-chest contact.

Bing, Bang, Bong 25

c) The arm wrap is solid.

d) Upon contact, the LB maintains a wide base with accelerated feet movement.

- Coaches like this drill for the high intensity created by having the LB pursue all three ball carriers.

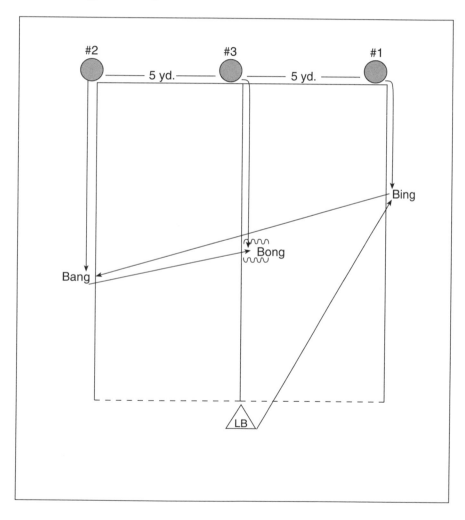

26 Shuffle to Crossover

Coach: Scott Pelluer
College: University of Washington
Head Coach: Jim Lambright

Purpose: To teach the use of inside-out leverage against the ball carrier while emphasizing the shuffle technique and appropriate use of the crossover run.

Procedure:

1. Holding a football, the ball carrier alternately jogs, runs, and walks from the sideline straight down a yard line to the hash mark.

2. The LB starts the drill by facing the ball carrier at a depth of five yards.

3. While working on a downfield track, the LB mirrors the movement of the ball carrier.

   a) If the ball carrier jogs or walks, the LB works downfield toward the ball carrier using a shuffle (S) technique.

   b) If the ball carrier runs, the LB works downfield toward the ball carrier using a crossover (CO) run.

4. The drill is completed when the ball carrier and LB meet at the hash mark.

Key Points:

- To start the drill, the LB aligns in a fundamental stance.

- It is essential that the LB keep moving toward the ball carrier by working downfield. He uses an inside-out technique.

- The LB must always be in a position to handle any cutback move by the ball carrier.

Shuffle to Crossover

26

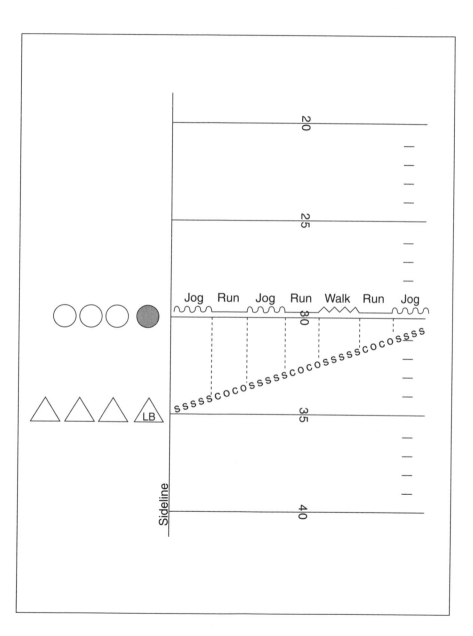

27   Door Tackle

Coach: Tim Rose
College: Minnesota
Head Coach: Jim Wacker

Purpose: To teach linebackers how to expand vision and to react to ball carriers on cutback plays.

Procedure:

1. A student manager holds up one end of an opaque door, wrestling mat, or four-by-eight piece of plywood toward the side of the ball carrier.

2. Place a cone one yard from both sides of the standing door.

3. At a depth of four yards, the ball carrier lines up behind the door with a football.

4. At a depth of four yards, the LB lines up in front of the door and one yard off to the side.

5. The drill begins when the LB starts shuffling behind the door.

6. When the ball carrier can't see the LB, he runs left or right between the door and the cone.

7. The LB, shuffling behind the door, reacts to the ball carrier by making a form tackle in the direction of the shuffle or opposite the shuffle, depending on which side the ball carrier runs.

Key Points:

- The ball carrier runs only between the door and cone.

- When the LB is out of sight, the ball carrier makes a choice to run right or left.

- When shuffling, teach the LB to keep his feet moving (alive), his head up, and his eyes focused.

- The LB makes a form tackle in the direction of the shuffle or on the cutback.

- This drill teaches LBs to tackle ball carriers when they show up in an unexpected hole.

Door Tackle

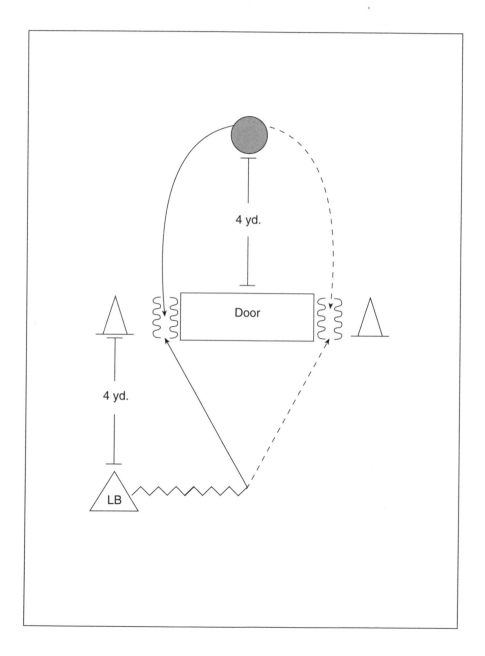

27

4 yd.

Door

4 yd.

LB

28 **Score Tackling**

Coach: Jerry Sandusky
College: Penn State University
Head Coach: Joe Paterno

Purpose: To teach linebacker movement and direction change before making a tackle.

Procedure:

1. Place five bags on the ground two yards apart, parallel to each other.
2. The ball carriers and LBs align on opposite sides of the middle bag.
3. The ball carrier begins the drill by running back and forth between the outside bags.
4. The LB mirrors the ball carrier by running on his side of the bags.
5. On the coach's command "score," the ball carrier runs up the nearest alley between two of the bags and attempts to get across the front edge of the bags.
6. The LB reacts by stepping between the bags to tackle the ball carrier. The LB squares up, attacks, and drives the ball carrier back.

Key Points:

- The ball carrier has the option to fake the LB while running between the bags.
- The LB keeps his feet moving laterally to square up with the ball carrier.
- The LB learns to change direction based on the ball carrier's running tempo.

Score Tackling

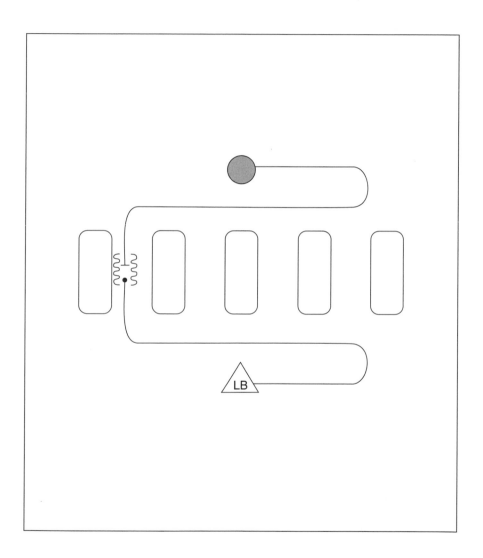

29   Drag

Coach: Jim Southward
College: Mississippi Delta Community College
Head Coach: Jim Southward

Purpose: To teach linebackers to recognize receivers running crossing or drag routes.

Procedure:

1. Give each receiver a designated route to run.
2. Use a fire hose to ensure proper alignment.
3. Both inside LBs align on the outside shoulder of the OGs, five yards deep.
4. On the coach's snap, all receivers come off the line of scrimmage. The LBs continue with normal pass drops.
5. When the LBs recognize crossing or drag routes, they establish verbal communication.

Key Points:

- Whenever a receiver crosses the face of a LB, the LB gives a loud "drag" call.
- The LB must make sure the receiver has crossed his face or left his hook area before making the drag call.
- Upon hearing the call, the other LB must stop his normal drop and find the receiver who is running the drag route. If necessary, the LB will come back to take that receiver.
- The LB making the drag call should continue to hunt for a second receiver in his area.
- The coach will use different formations so that the LBs can practice making on-field adjustments to routes, timing, and so forth.

Drag

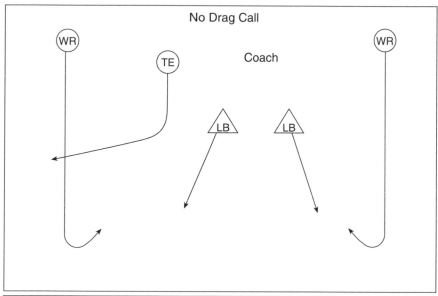

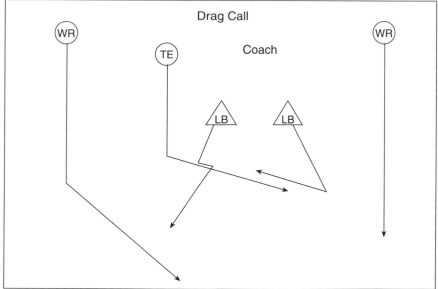

30 Lateral Mirror Tackle

Coach: Stephen Spagnuolo
College: Rutgers University
Head Coach: Doug Graber

Purpose: To teach linebackers to stay in tempo with the ball carrier, to eliminate a cutback by the ball carrier, and to execute a proper angle tackle.

Procedure:

1. Place one cone on a hash mark; place the second cone five yards wider.
2. The ball carrier and LB align five yards apart on the sideline.
3. The ball carrier faces the hash mark. The LB faces the ball carrier.
4. The drill begins on the ball carrier's movement across the field. He should alternate his tempo by executing a slow jog or full sprint until he reaches the hash mark.
5. The LB mirrors the ball carrier's speed with a shuffle or crossover lateral run.
6. At the hash mark, the ball carrier either cuts back inside or runs outside between the cones.
7. Near the hash mark, the LB attacks the ball carrier and executes an angle tackle versus the cutback or outside run.

Key Points:

- When the ball carrier is in full sprint, the LB should use the crossover run technique.
- Throughout the drill, the LB must stay low with his shoulders square to the line of scrimmage until he tackles the ball carrier.
- Throughout the drill, coach the LB to lag one yard behind the ball carrier for the cutback.

Lateral Mirror Tackle

30

- Coaching points on angle tackling: On contact, get the head across, accelerate the feet, and "hit through the ball carrier."

- Variations to the drill: At the beginning, add a blocker or big ball that the LB must defeat with a low block. Another choice is to add agile bags in the LB's path.

- The drill can be run in both directions.

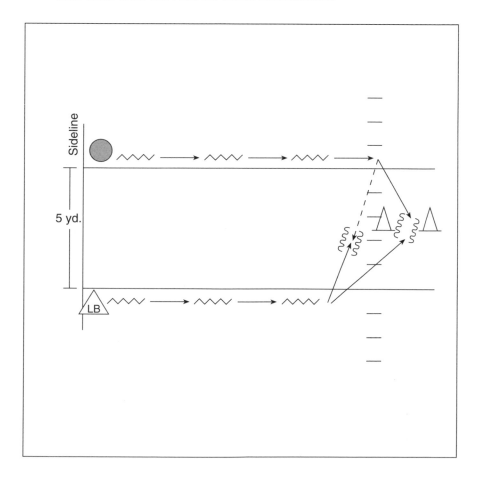

31   Form Tackle

Coach: Mike Toop
College: University of Pennsylvania
Head Coach: Al Bagnoli

Purpose: To teach and emphasize proper tackling technique.

Procedure:

1. At a depth of five yards, the tackler faces the ball carrier, who is holding a shield on his side.
2. The coach stands behind the tackler and, within a designated five-yard area, signals to the ball carrier which direction to run.
3. On the ball carrier's movement, the tackler attacks the ball carrier and executes a form tackle.
4. Just before the tackler makes contact, the ball carrier lets go of the shield. The tackler must pin the shield to the ball carrier.
5. Two lines of tacklers and ball carriers wait to the side for their turns.

Key Points:

- Using proper balance, the tackler must execute correct tackling technique to ignite shock contact with power and follow through on the shield.
- To ensure a chest-to-chest tackle and follow-through, the tackler must roll his hips into the ball carrier and keep driving his legs.
- To pin the shield with a chest-to-chest tackle, the tackler must keep his head up and slide his head to the side.
- A point of emphasis is that the tackler must keep his arms within the plane of his body and wrap them under the ball carrier's armpits.
- A variation is to put a mat behind the ball carrier so that the LB can execute a full tackle.

Form Tackle

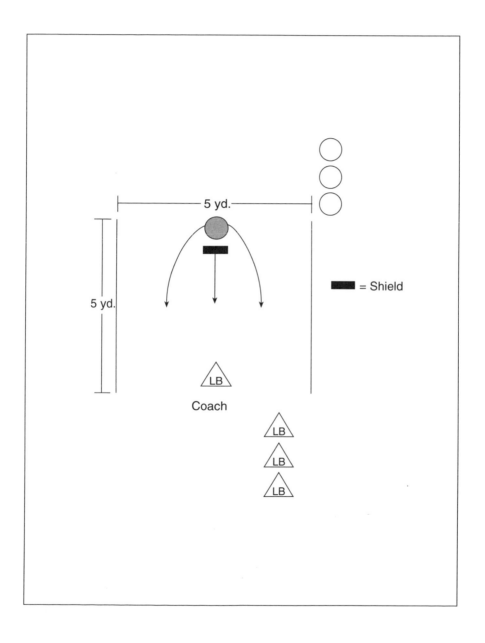

32   3-on-1

Coach: Kurt Van Valkenburgh
College: University of Hawaii

Purpose: To teach a linebacker how to defeat the base block and angle block while executing the attack and rip technique.

Procedure:

1. Align three blockers three yards apart on a straight line.
2. The LB, who is slightly backed off, aligns on the middle blocker.
3. On command, the middle blocker executes a base block on the LB.
4. The LB defeats the base block and shuffles left to the second blocker.
5. The LB defeats the angle block of the second blocker and shuffles right to the third blocker.
6. The LB defeats the downfield block by the third blocker and penetrates across the line of scrimmage.

Key Points:

- The LB explodes out of his stance versus the middle blocker. He must control the base block and must lock out his arms before shuffling. The key coaching point is proper explosion.
- The LB attacks the outside half of the angle blocker to turn him. The explosion should place the LB's head on the outside numbers. His left arm should be locked out.
- Against the downfield block, the LB uses a rip technique. He lowers his hips, places his backside shoulder under the armpit of the blocker, and rips his backside arm and leg through.
- The LB uses the rip technique to cross the blocker's face and to cross the line of scrimmage with quick steps.
- The RB may be added. After the LB executes the rip technique, he can make a tackle.

3-on-1

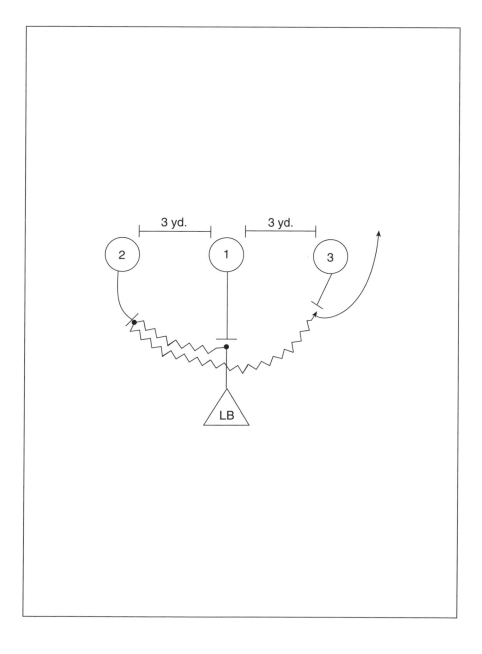

PART 3
Defensive Back Drills

I t's fitting that one of the positions in the defensive backfield is called "safety." Defensive backs are the last line of defense for keeping an opponent out of the end zone. "Don't give up the big play" is foremost in their minds. They know that one mistake means 6 points for the opposition—and a negative reaction from coaches to screaming fans!

But learning and playing the defensive back position is not about avoiding the negative; it's about being aggressive in stopping the long run and defending the pass. A defensive back can best accomplish these tasks if he possesses the following attributes:

- Considerable athletic talent
- Eagerness to make hits and big plays
- Plenty of smarts
- Toughness to survive the inevitable—getting beat for a TD

To play a defensive backfield position effectively a player must have speed and jumping ability to get to the ball quickly. Then, once at the point of attack, the defensive back must make the hit or interception to stop the play. Defensive backs must also have the mental skills to make reads and not be duped by the trickery of the offense. Deion Sanders gets much publicity and attention for his nonfootball theatrics, but what makes him an exceptional defensive back is that he possesses all the qualities you look for in a cornerback.

Whether playing man, zone, nickel, or dime, defensive backs must make many adjustments and fill many roles. The two primary labels for defensive back positions, safety and cornerback, apply only on the broadest terms. A strong safety may differ as much from a free safety as the free safety differs from a teammate playing cornerback. But it's helpful to have in mind general characteristics to look for when filling these positions in the defensive backfield.

It is part of the role of safeties to roam in the center and to help their counterparts, the corners, with deep routes. As the last guardians of the goal post, their work is cut out for them. Asked to play man or to anchor the zone, a defensive safety must be prepared to react to any ball carrier who crosses the line of scrimmage. Toughness and courage highlight their calling cards.

Cornerbacks of the '90s are often asked to play man coverage behind the pressure tactics of the front seven. If they do it right, they disrupt receivers' routes and stick to them like glue through their patterns. Occasionally, a corner will be asked to surprise the opponent by sneaking in on a blitz and chasing down the quarterback. And when a runner gets loose around end and into the secondary, cornerbacks must be prepared to knock the back out-of-bounds or make the sure open-field tackle.

Defensive coaches probably spend more time choosing defensive backs than players at any other position. It isn't an easy task to find great cover men who can make game-saving tackles in the open field. In part 3 of *AFCA's Defensive Football Drills* defensive secondary coaches share the drills they use to prepare defensive backs to perform these difficult tasks successfully in games.

Defensive Back Drills

Drill	Coach	Program
33 Hands	Chris Ball	Western Oregon State
34 Partner Weave	Tim Beckman	Western Carolina
35 Triangle Block	Jerry Brown	Northwestern University
36 Playing the Pass	Andy Christoff	Colorado
37 Zone Break	Ron Collins	Washington University
38 Cover 2 Stretcher	Robert D. Cope	Baylor
39 Gauntlet	Steve Davis	Troy State
40 Big M	Phil Elmassian	Boston College
41 Break W	Paul Ferraro	Bowling Green
42 Clap (Man Coverage)	Jon Heacock	Youngstown State
43 Interception Return	Larry Kerr	Colorado State
44 Ballhawk	Rocky Long	UCLA
45 Verticals	Jeff Mills	Idaho
46 Square	Mike Phillips	Hardin-Simmons
47 Downfield Block	Joel Quattrone	Dickinson (Pennsylvania)
48 Break Cushion	Rick Smith	Kentucky
49 Zone Drop	Don Smolyn	Lenape H.S. (New Jersey)
50 Hash Mark Tip	Ron Zook	Florida

33 Hands

Coach: Chris Ball
College: Western Oregon State
Head Coach: Blaine Bennett

Purpose: To read the WR's hands to know when to close and look for the ball.

Procedure:
1. WR aligns 8-12 yards from the sideline with DB aligned one yard inside and three yards behind.
2. The QB (or coach) aligns 10-12 yards from the two players on the line of scrimmage.
3. On command, one set of WR and DB releases downfield.
4. Within 15 yards, the QB throws the ball to the WR's outside shoulder.
5. The WR fades away from the DB when the ball is thrown.
6. The DB closes the gap between himself and the WR by reading the WR's hands—not by looking for the ball.

Key Points:
- The WR will tip off the location of the ball by his hand placement.
- DB's inside hand should be between the WR and the ball.
- If the ball is caught, the DB should strip the ball with his inside hand.
- The DB must make sure his opposite hand and arm are in position to make a tackle if the ball is caught by the receiver.
- DB should not look at the ball until he closes the gap, and he is in a position to make a play on the ball.

Hands

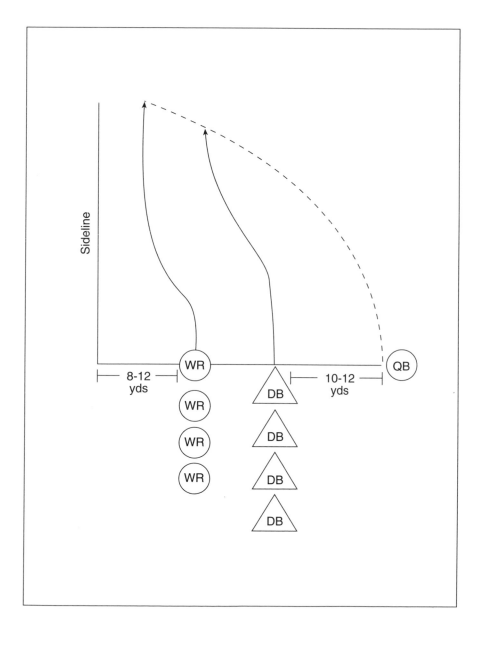

34 Partner Weave

Coach: Tim Beckman
College: Western Carolina University
Head Coach: Steve Hodgin

Purpose: To teach and practice fundamentals, techniques, and ability to keep the proper width and depth cushion on an opposing receiver.

Procedure:

1. The receiver aligns on the designated line of scrimmage.
2. Proper alignment for the DB keys the hip of the receiver.
3. On the coach's command, the receiver stems at a slight angle to the right while running at three-quarters speed downfield.
4. The DB backpedals, keeping a designated width and depth cushion on the receiver.
5. After running five yards downfield, the receiver works back at a slight angle to his left.
6. At this time, the DB points his hips toward the new angle and keeps a proper width and depth cushion on the receiver.
7. The receiver repeats, running right at a slight angle. The DB repeats his technique, keeping a proper width and depth cushion on the receiver.
8. After running right, the receiver runs the vertical route.
9. After the DB loses his two-yard cushion, he throws his head and shoulder into the receiver.

Key Points:

- Teach the DB coverage hip, which is to key on the hip of the receiver.
- Throughout the drill, the DB must always key the coverage hip.
- Also, the DB always works to maintain a proper width and depth cushion on the receiver.

Partner Weave

- When the cushion is broken, the DB throws his head and shoulders into the receiver, placing a short jab on the coverage hip to close on the receiver.
- This will naturally open the hips and prevent separation from the receiver.

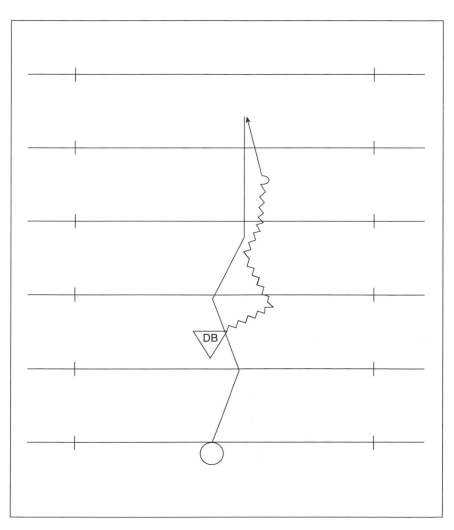

35   Triangle Block

Coach: Jerry Brown
College: Northwestern University
Head Coach: Gary Barnett

Purpose: To teach CBs to defeat WRs' downfield blocks and force ball carriers outside; to teach DSs to track the ball carrier inside out; to teach the backside DC proper backside pursuit.

Procedure:

1. DBs align in a three-deep look; CB s 7-9 yards off each WR and the hole safety about 12 yards deep. Align WR s to the right and left of the QB (or coach). The ball carrier aligns seven yards behind the QB to receive the pitch.
2. To begin the drill, the DB coach standing behind the DBs points the direction for the ball carrier's sweep.
3. As the ball is pitched, the WRs come off to block, and the DBs simulate their pass-run reads.
4. After identifying the run, the CB reacts to defeat the WR's downfield block, containing the run and forcing the ball carrier inside. Or he tackles the ball carrier, if the ball carrier runs outside.
5. If the ball carrier runs inside, the hole safety makes the tackle while the backside CB is in a good pursuit position.

Key Points:

- Work in groups of three and occasionally keep DBs honest by having the QB pass to the WRs.
- If the WR stalk blocks, the CB (with his outside arm free) squares up, drops his hips, and attacks with a two-hand shiver to the chest using an extra push from the outside arm.
- If the WR cut blocks, the CB uses a push technique to stifle the WR's throwing motion. With the open palm nearest to the WR, the CB will push the WR's head away. With the other arm, he pushes down on the WR's near shoulder to put him on the ground.

Triangle Block 35

- If the ball carrier runs inside, the inside-out tracking DS who maintains a slight inside position on the ball carrier comes up to tackle head across the front numbers.
- The tackler forms up the ball carrier while the second and third defenders punch or strip the ball.

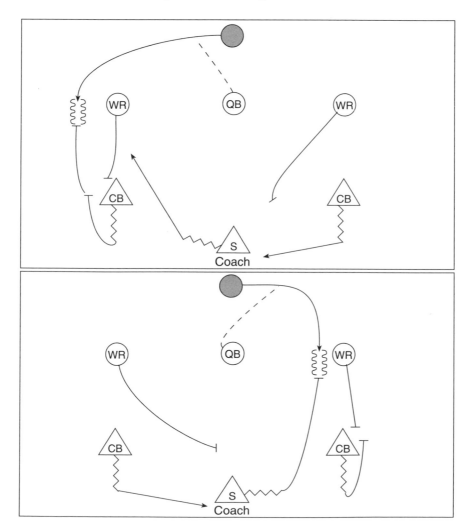

36   Playing the Pass

Coach: Andy Christoff
College: University of Colorado
Head Coach: Rick Neuheisel

Purpose: To develop the techniques necessary to play the pass, with an emphasis on desire, speed, and concentration.

Procedure:

1. Prior to the drill, the DB must master the backpedal, must be able to change directions, and must be able to recognize pass patterns.
2. To start the drill, the DB lines up on a receiver in man coverage.
3. The WR runs an out, in, or go pattern, and the DB plays the ball.

Key Points:

- In man coverage, the DB always keeps eye contact on the receiver while looking for the ball. The DB must never look away from the receiver.
- If unable to make an interception or deflect the pass, the DB will tear away the upfield arm of the receiver. This is the arm farthest from the flight of the ball.
- The DB knows that an incomplete pass gains no yards, which is a plus.
- The coach emphasizes that each player should be the best at his position, maintain peak condition, and know his responsibility.

Playing the Pass

36

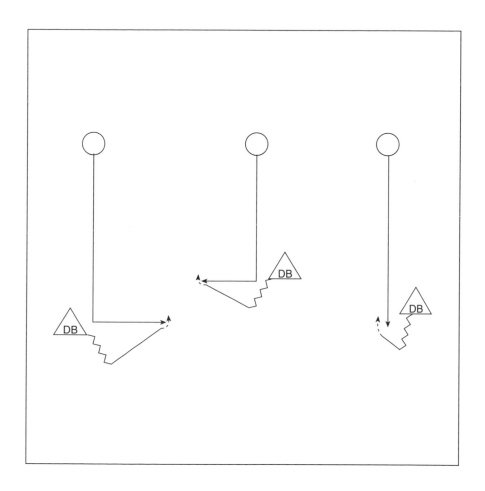

37   Zone Break

Coach: Ron Collins
College: Washington University
Head Coach: Larry Kindbom

Purpose: To teach the proper fundamentals for reading the QB, to anticipate the ball, and to gain confidence while covering two receivers within a zone.

Procedure:

1. As a stationary WR aligns on each hash mark, the DB splits the distance between them.
2. The QB (coach), aligns 15 yards directly in front of the DB.
3. On ball movement, the QB takes a three to five step drop. At the same time the DB pedals straight back.
4. As the QB sets, he will turn his eyes and shoulders towards a WR.
5. The DB reads the QB by checking his eyes and shoulders.
6. As the QB's free hand comes off the ball, the DB plants, drives, intercepts the ball, tucks it, and sprints past the QB.

Key Points:

- Emphasize correct stance and proper backpedaling technique while the DB reads the QB.
- On the break, the DB's eyes are on the WR. After acceleration, his eyes are on the ball.
- Coach the DB to gain ground as quickly as possible to avoid taking false steps.
- The DB looks the ball all the way in. He catches it at its highest point with both hands.

Zone Break

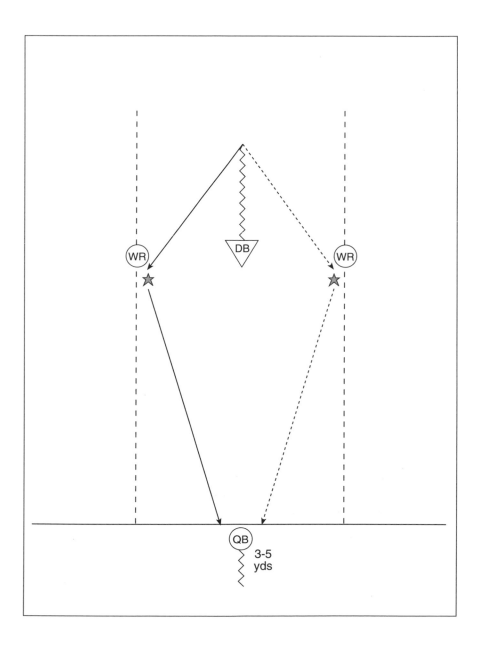

38 Cover 2 Stretcher

Coach: Robert D. Cope
College: Baylor University
Head Coach: Chuck Reedy

Purpose: To use the vertical stretch and the high-low principles while attacking two-deep coverage.

Procedure:

1. There are five receivers in the drill.
   a) A receiver aligns at each sideline on the 40-yard line. The receivers release outside and run down the sideline.
   b) A receiver aligns at each hash mark, two yards deeper than the outside receiver. They push off three yards and run into the flat.
   c) A fifth receiver aligns ahead of the QB on the 40-yard line in the middle of the field. He runs straight down the field.
2. The secondary aligns in cover 2. The CBs cover the outside receivers. The safeties cover the hash mark receivers.
3. The QB starts the drill by executing a five-step drop and by throwing to one of the receivers.

Key Points:

- Each safety must contend with the outside receiver on his side and the middle receiver when both are running deep.
  a) To defend the vertical stretch, each safety must get depth on the hash mark.
  b) Safeties must read the QB and be ready to break in the direction of the throw.
  c) Teach safeties to break downhill on everything.

- Each CB has a boundary route with a receiver in front.
  a) The CB learns to funnel and sink, which helps to protect the boundary.
  b) Teach the CB to drive up on the flat route.

Cover 2 Stretcher

38

- Variations of the drill include a seven-step drop by the QB and having coverage intercept the thrown ball.

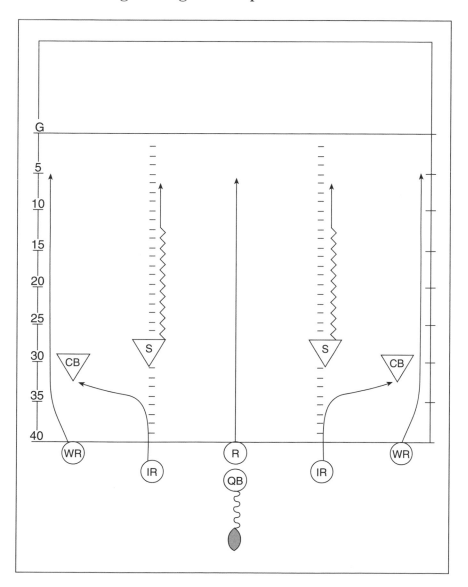

39 Gauntlet

Coach: Steve Davis
College: Troy State University
Head Coach: Larry Blakeney

Purpose: To develop proper open-field tackling skills for DBs.

Procedure:

1. Align defenders in three lines, five yards apart.
2. The first defender in each line stands between two cones set five yards apart.
3. Place two more cones downfield five yards apart.
4. One ball carrier faces the first defender, five yards away.
5. On the coach's command, the ball carrier tries to run by the defender.
6. If the defender tackles the ball carrier, another ball carrier executes the drill.
7. If the ball carrier runs by the first defender, he regroups to run at a second defender.
8. If the second defender tackles the ball carrier, the drill begins with a new ball carrier.
9. If the ball carrier runs by the second defender, he regroups to run at a third defender.
10. The third defender tries to tackle the ball carrier.

Key Points:

- Before switching, each defender has two attempts to tackle a ball carrier.
- The ball carriers can be running backs and receivers who are likely to be in the open field.
- Conduct this competitive drill at full speed.
- Emphasize proper open-field tackling technique with head up and helmet across the runner's numbers.
- To work on open-field angle tackling, the defender aligns at one of the cones.

Gauntlet

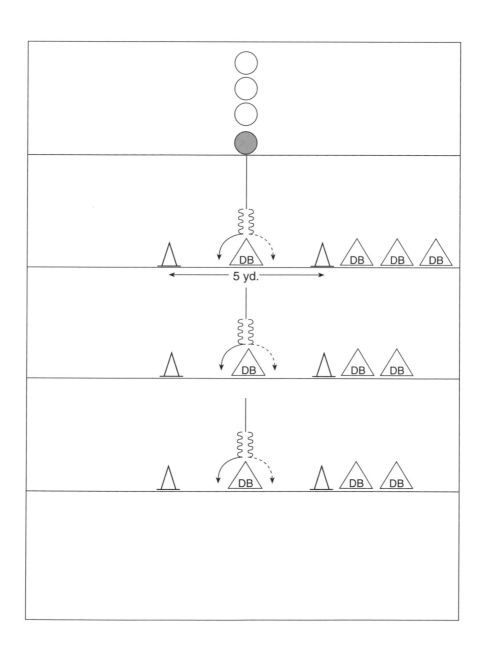

5 yd.

40   **Big M**

Coach: Phil Elmassian
College: Boston College
Head Coach: Dan Henning

Purpose: To improve change of direction for DBs coming to and going away from LOS with emphasis on footwork efficiency.

Procedure:

1. The DB faces the coach (with ball) and executes a backward run.
2. At a predetermined depth, the DB changes direction by breaking left toward the line of scrimmage at a 45-degree angle.
3. At the line of scrimmage, the DB changes direction by breaking left at a 45-degree angle to a predetermined depth.
4. At the predetermined depth, the DB changes direction by coming directly to the line of scrimmage.

Key Points:

- The drill begins with good backward run technique.
- Footwork efficiency calls for the DB controlling his footwork and keeping his feet underneath.
- Emphasize shortening stride length and decreasing arm movement when changing direction.
- During the drill, the DB must focus and keep his eyes on the ball.

Big M

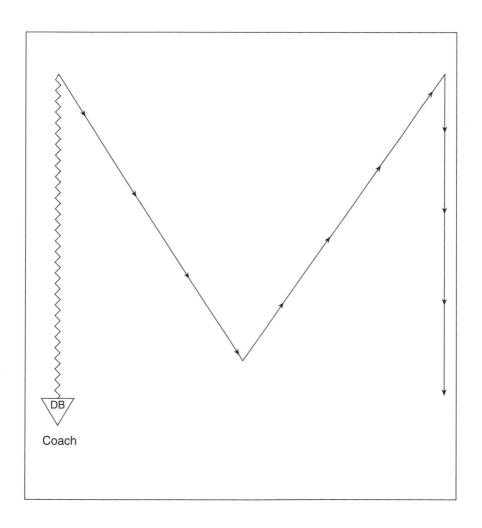

41 Break W

Coach: Paul Ferraro
College: Bowling Green State University
Head Coach: Gary Blackney

Purpose: To develop a technique for defensive backs to change direction once in the backpedal, breaking both with and away from their bodies.

Procedure:

1. The DBs form one line. While facing the coach at the 5-yard line, one DB at a time aligns on the sideline.
2. The drill starts with the DB pedaling backward.
3. On the coach's command, the DB opens his hips to the left, turns into a crossover run, and breaks toward the sideline at the 10-yard line.
4. Repeat the drill on the 10-yard line. This time, the DB opens his hips to the right, turns into a crossover run, and breaks to the sideline at the 15-yard line.
5. Repeat the drill on the 15-yard line. Eventually the DB works back to the 5-yard line. When repeating the drill, the DB starts by first opening his hips to the right and then to the left.
6. End the drill with a second reaction. Second reactions could include recovering a fumble, making a tackle, or intercepting a pass.

Key Points:

- Throughout the drill, the DB must stay at the same level. He should avoid starting low and rising up.
- To change direction, the DB's feet must stay within the framework of his body.
- The coach insists that the DB break on command. This emphasizes a gamelike condition.
- Always have a second reaction at the end of the drill.

Break W

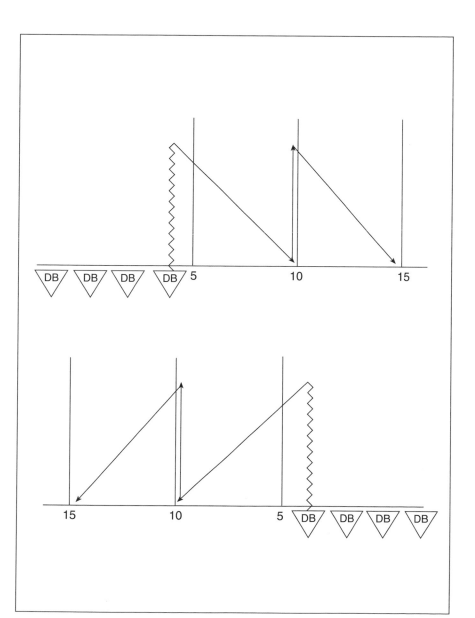

42 Clap (Man Coverage)

Coach: Jon Heacock
College: Youngstown State University
Head Coach: Jim Tressel

Purpose: To teach defensive backs in man-to-man coverage a technique to separate the ball from a receiver.

Procedure:
1. Pair up the DB and WR side by side on a yard line.
2. On the same yard line, the coach (QB) aligns in the middle of the field.
3. The WR (with ball) begins to run a vertical fade route.
4. The DB follows in tight hip pocket phase with his back to the QB and his eyes on the WR.
5. After running five to six yards downfield, the WR extends both hands up to the ball.
6. The DB reacts to the outstretched arms of the WR by "clapping" the WR's outside arm with the arm closest to the QB. The DB should separate the football from the receiver.
7. As the DB and WR return to their opposite lines, the next pair comes up.

Key Points:
- Confine the drill to a limited area so that the coach can evaluate technique.
- When the DB claps with the arm farthest from the receiver, it naturally pulls him closer to the receiver. This should result in separation of the ball.
- The DB places himself in position to separate the ball from the receiver.
- Enhance the drill by having the QB throw the short fade route.

Clap (Man Coverage)

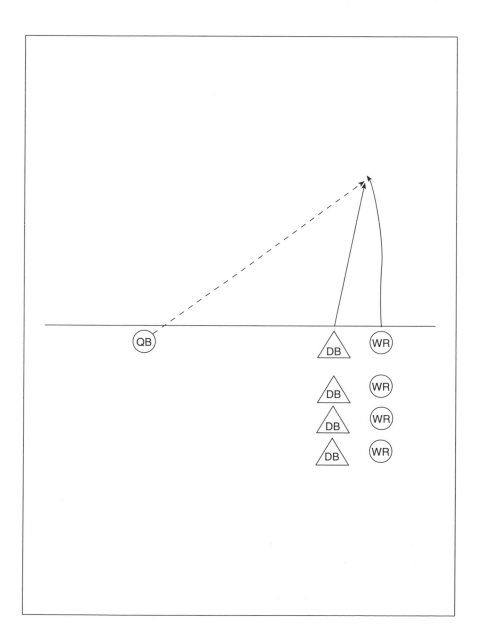

43 **Interception Return**

Coach: Larry Kerr
College: Colorado State
Head Coach: Sonny Lubick

Purpose: To teach players a scheme which is designed to obtain the maximum return yards on each interception.

Procedure:

1. Place two cones 3-5 yards outside the normal TE alignment, and place another two cones 5-7 yards deep behind them.

2. The TE, OC, and QB align according to the formation called.

3. The team huddles, receives a defensive call, breaks, recognizes the offensive formation, and communicates the on-field adjustments.

4. At the snap, the DL rushes the passer; LBs and DBs drop into the coverage call. The QB throws the ball downfield to any coverage back.

5. After the interception, the DL, LBs, and DBs head to the near sideline and form a wall. Each man blocks his nearest opponent.

6. The returner intercepts the ball at its highest point, then runs with the ball to the near sideline.

Key Points:

- While the DL key on the ball, the LBs and DBs key on the backfield action.

- After an interception, the nearest DL blocks the QB and the nearest DB blocks the intended receiver.

- Emphasize that the returner must take the ball to the near sideline, where the blockers will set a wall. Blockers must immediately assume that the return will go to the near sideline. This will help develop a caravan and eliminate clips.

- Stress that players should not block below the waist nor block behind the interceptor.

Interception Return

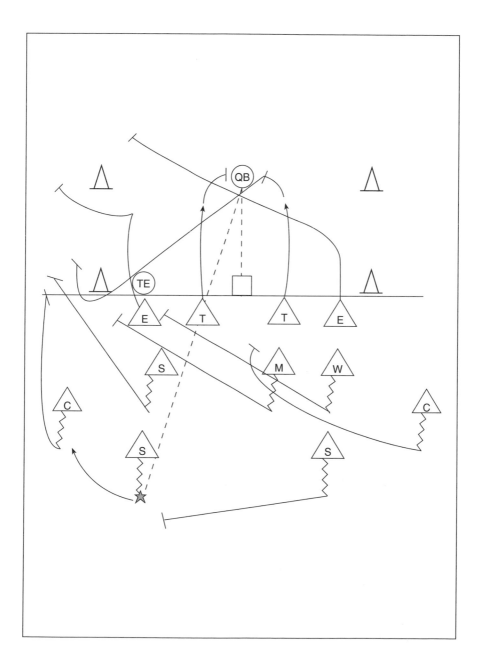

Ballhawk

Coach: Rocky Long
College: UCLA
Head Coach: Bob Toledo

Purpose: To teach or improve defensive back techniques for body control, change of direction, and footwork and to teach defensive backs how to finish with an interception.

Procedure:

1. In sequence, teach the following DB techniques.
   a) Backpedal and plant
   b) Ninety-degree out break
   c) Vertical run
   d) Forty-five-degree post break
   e) Post-corner break

2. Start the drill by having the DBs form a line. One DB at a time faces the coach.

3. As the coach shows the ball, the DB calls "pass," and starts to pedal backward.

4. When the coach turns his shoulders and points with the ball, the player should turn his hips in the same direction at a predetermined angle.

5. As the player reaches speed, the coach turns his shoulders and points the ball in the opposite direction. The player should turn his hips and change direction.

6. As the player reaches speed, the coach pumps.

7. The player plants, and as he accelerates back toward the coach at full speed, yells "ball."

8. Without slowing down, the player intercepts the thrown ball and runs it back to the coach.

Key Points:

- The DB must keep his eyes on the QB (coach) except when executing a speed turn.

- During the post-corner break, the DB uses a speed-turn technique in which he whips his head and shoulders around, turning his back on the coach.

Ballhawk

- Throughout the drill, the DB maintains a low base and keeps his shoulders over his toes.
- The coach looks for and corrects flaws in technique at each movement—the pedal, stride, change, break, and intercept.
- Have the DB accelerate on all cuts back to the line of scrimmage and intercept at full speed.

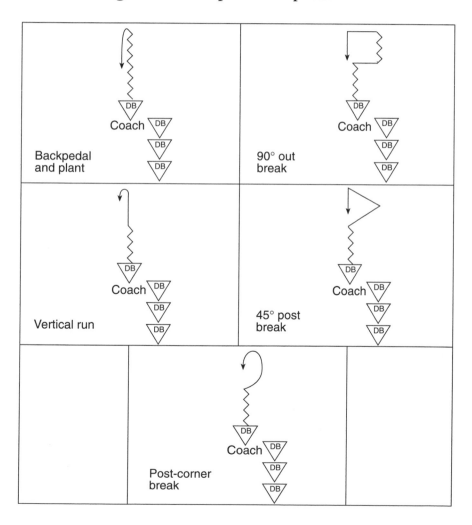

Verticals

Coach: Jeff Mills
College: Idaho
Head Coach: Chris Tormey

Purpose: To teach corners how to play vertical routes in the deep outside one-third zone and to defend four vertical pass patterns with the safeties.

Procedure:

1. Align the first receiver on top of the number. He releases downfield and runs an outside route. As the ball is thrown, the CB executes a zone drop to defend the vertical route to the outside.

2. The second receiver aligns on the hash mark. He releases downfield and runs a seam route. The CB overlaps with the DS when the ball is thrown to an inside vertical route.

3. The third receiver aligns on the other hash mark before running a seam route downfield. The DS aligns in the middle. As the receiver releases, the DS backpedals to the middle of his zone.

4. Finally, a fourth receiver aligns on top of the opposite number. As the ball is thrown, the CB executes a zone drop to defend the outside third.

Key Points:

- The DBs maintain a five yard cushion on all receivers.
  - a) If the cushion is broken, the CB opens to the inside and keep his eyes on the QB.
  - b) If the DS cushion is broken, the DS opens to the side where the QB's head and shoulder are leading.
- The CB backpedals full speed toward the top of the numbers at an angle.
- The DS backpedals full speed to the middle of the field.
- The DB overlaps on a ball thrown to the inside vertical, intercepts the ball at its highest point, and returns it up the nearest sideline.

Verticals

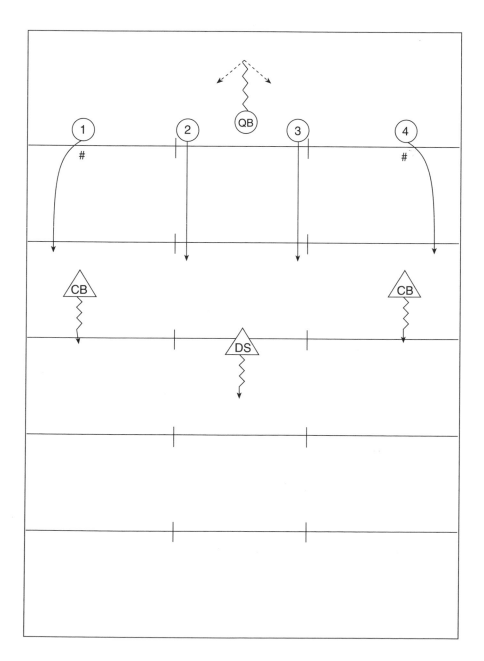

46   Square

Coach: Mike Phillips
College: Hardin-Simmons University
Head Coach: Jimmie Keeling

Purpose: To teach cornerbacks the fundamentals for man-to-man coverage.

Procedure:

1. The teaching station consists of a 25-yard square on the field.

2. Use the sideline as one side of the square. Complete the square by placing four vertical lines 5 yards apart.

3. Three lines of receivers line up on the 10-yard line. The first line is 5 yards from the sideline. The remaining two lines are 10 yards apart.

4. The cornerback makes sure he is properly aligned on the receiver and in a proper defensive stance.

5. The receiver runs a chosen route at the CB.

6. The CB reacts to the route run by the receiver by backpedaling and maintaining a cushion of 2 to 3 yards.

Key Points:

- The CB learns to plant and drive on an interception line to the ball.

- Coaches insist on the CB driving on an intercept line and not following the receiver.

- At the point of interception, the CB always has his upfield arm free to tackle with, which leaves the arm closest to the ball free to knock down the pass.

- The CB is constantly reminded to accelerate on the break.

- Because the lines are spaced apart, more than one receiver can go at the same time.

Square

46

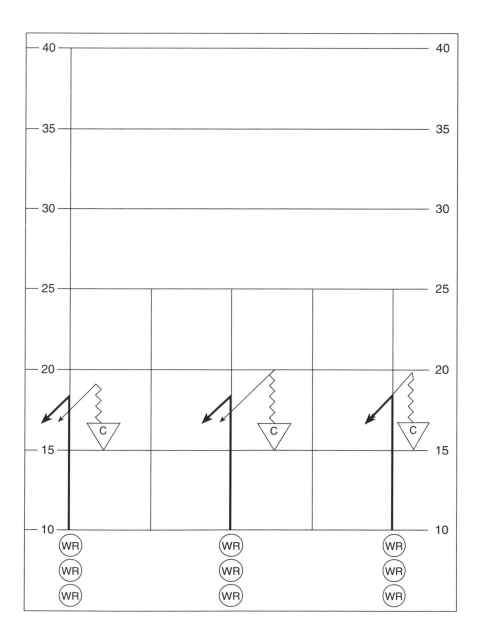

47 Downfield Block

Coach: Joel Quattrone
College: Dickinson College (Pennsylvania)
Head Coach: Darwin Breaux

Purpose: To teach DBs techniques to defeat a stalk block by the wide receiver.

Procedure:

1. Three offensive players are in the drill.
   a) The QB is on the hash mark with the ball.
   b) The ball carrier is behind the QB at a depth of seven yards.
   c) The WR splits the distance between the normal TE split (bag on ground) and the sideline.
2. Space four cones three yards apart, forming an angle from the end of the bag downfield toward the sideline.
3. The DB aligns on the WR at a predetermined width and depth.
4. The drill begins when the QB turns and pitches the ball back to the ball carrier.
5. The WR comes out to stalk block the DB.
6. The DB must read the path of the ball carrier and make his play on the stalk block accordingly.
7. The DB must defeat the stalk block and form tackle the ball carrier.

Key Points:

- The DB must take proper read steps while deciding whether the play is a run or pass. One variation is to have the QB drop back and throw the ball.
- Once the keys have dictated a run response, the DB should aggressively attack the stalk block from the outside in.
- The use of the outside-in technique keeps the DB from being pinned inside and forces the ball carrier to run inside where there is team pursuit.

Downfield Block

47

- The DB attempts to get beyond the stalk block by using a "swim" or "rip" technique.
- If the DB neutralizes the stalk block, he must make the tackle coming off the receiver's block.
- It's important that the DB not allow the WR to turn his hips in any direction and give the ball carrier a running lane.

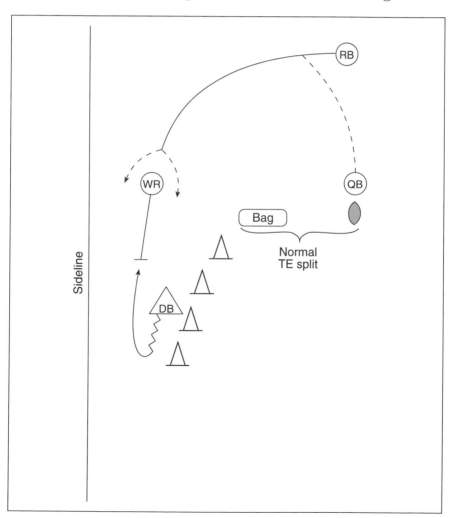

48   Break Cushion

Coach: Rick Smith
College: University of Kentucky
Head Coach: Bill Curry

Purpose: To teach cornerbacks when to get out of their shuffle, when to turn and run with the receiver, and how to play the long ball.

Procedure:

1. Receivers line up on one sideline and face the other sideline.
2. The receiver runs a fly pattern down the yard line.
3. The CB aligns on the inside, seven to eight yards from the receiver.
4. The coach positions himself in the middle of the field with a football.
5. After the receiver and CB pass by the coach, the ball is thrown.

Key Points:

- One point of emphasis is to teach the CB when to get out of his shuffle technique.
- Once the CB turns and runs with the receiver, he should be looking for the long ball.
- If the receiver breaks the CB's cushion and is still facing inside, the CB turns and runs with the receiver.
- If the CB is in cloud technique coverage, add safeties to play the deep pattern.

Break Cushion

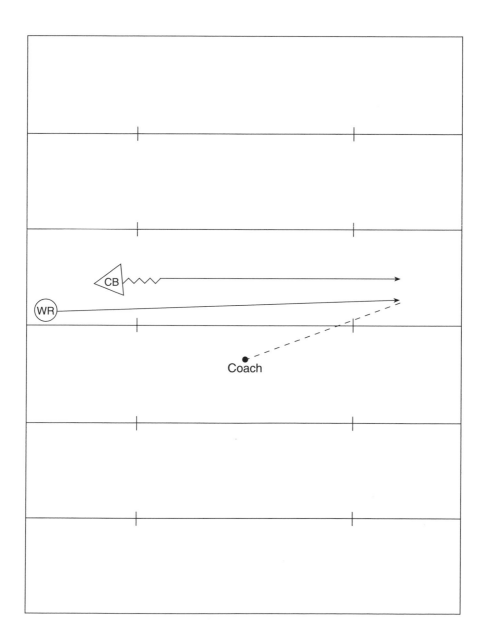

48

Zone Drop

Coach: Donald Smolyn
College: Lenape Valley Regional High School
(New Jersey)
Head Coach: Donald Smolyn

Purpose: To reinforce defensive back play on a pass within the concept of three-deep zone coverage.

Procedure:

1. Designate the line of scrimmage by a spacing hose.
2. At each sideline, place a cone 9 yards from the boundary and 22 yards deep. Place one cone 25 yards deep in the middle third.
3. To set up the drill, the three-deep secondary take their proper alignment, get in a good stance, and make the correct strength call based on a signal from the coach.
4. The coach (ball) aligns in the middle of the space hose. The coach snaps the ball and the three-deep secondary execute read steps.
5. After the players execute their read steps, the coach raises the ball to signify a pass play.
6. Upon seeing the ball raised, the players backpedal quickly to the zone cone.

Key Points:

- To reinforce the read step technique, players execute that skill longer in the drill than for a normal play.
- The three-deep must communicate a strength and pass call.
- With speed to the cone, players use the proper backpedal technique every time.
- Perform the drill from both hash marks and the middle of the field. Each three-deep group completes the drill before moving to another location.
- This drill is part of every defensive practice.

Zone Drop

49

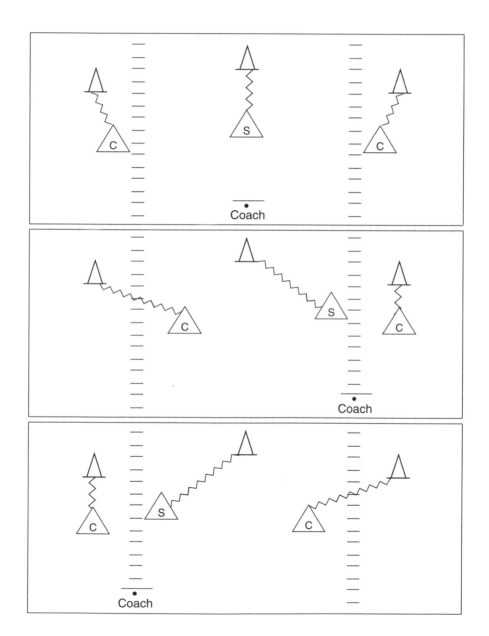

50   **Hash Mark Tip**

Coach: Ron Zook
College: University of Florida
Head Coach: Steve Spurrier

Purpose: To teach defensive backs to intercept tipped balls by reacting to a ball thrown to the opposite side of the field.

Procedure:

1. Place one receiver on each sideline with two DBs on each hash mark, 15 yards deep.
2. The coach stands between the hash marks.
3. When executing the drill, both receivers sprint downfield on command.
4. The DBs react by sprinting back. They must maintain a 5-yard cushion on the receivers.
5. Both DBs break toward the ball in the direction it is thrown.
6. The first defender tips the ball while the other one catches it in the air.

Key Points:

- Teach the DB to tip the ball at its highest point.
- After the catch, both DBs turn upfield and sprint to score.
- By watching the coach step to throw, both DBs know in which direction to break.
- The cushion must remain constant on the receivers.
- The DB who makes the catch will come from the opposite hash mark.

Hash Mark Tip

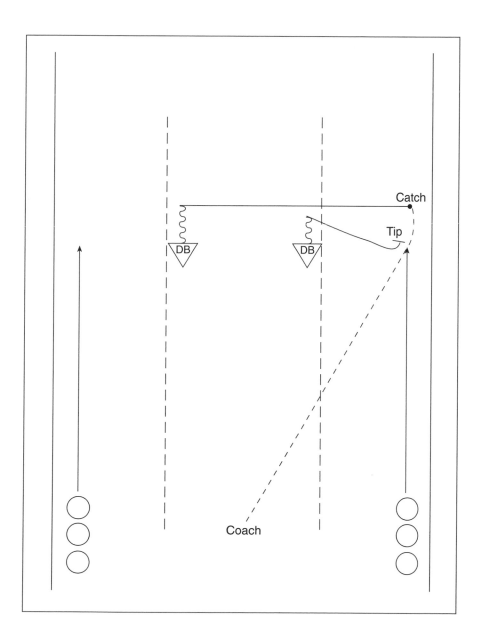

PART 4

Team Drills

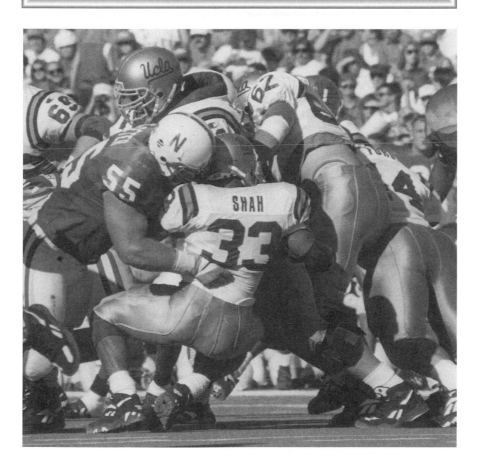

Good team defense is still the cornerstone of championship football. But today's attacking defenses rely on more speed and muscle than was the case when "contain" was the aim. Penetration, down-and-distance situations, and multiple formations now take priority over time of possession.

Many defensive coordinators are preaching an even more aggressive philosophy—turning the defense into the dictator, not the responder, creating turnovers to produce points and great field position. Some teams are as concerned about the number of takeaways they get as they are the number of yards they give up. First downs? Who cares, as long as they strip or intercept the ball before the offense can put points on the board.

The emphasis has changed from merely stopping the offense to exploiting and capitalizing on it. The "big-play" defense is what many believe to be the answer to the big-play offenses that are so common in today's game.

Last decade's switch to more down-and-distance specialization had another big impact in how team defense is played. Instead of simply lining up the same 11 players each snap to stop the offense, teams now use the 11 players best suited to handle the situation, formation, opponent, and even field conditions. Situational substitution has quickly gone from fad to fact of life.

Given the diversity and sophistication of offenses, it's truly amazing to find defenses that can handle every opponent throughout the season. One week they'll face the spread. The next, the option. Then the short passing game. And on and on. How can you possibly prepare for all these offensive schemes, not to mention the multiple formations, quick counts, and no-huddle attacks they'll throw at you?

It takes more than scouting reports, video analysis, and chalk talks. It takes solid fundamentals, starting with team pursuit and tackling skills. Remember, there's no limit on how many players can tackle the ball carrier or pull down the receiver. The more, the better.

Although the philosophy may have changed, two principles remain in any solid defensive plan: Stop the run and pressure the quarterback.

The drills in this section stress both the old basics—team pursuit and tackling—and the new attacking defensive styles. Performed with all-out effort and correct technique, these drills will develop a formidable team defensive attack. Follow the instructions and tips provided by the outstanding coaches who donated the drills, and you'll get the results you're looking for from your defensive squad.

Team Drills

Drill	Coach	Program
51 Open Field	Will Bowman	Toledo
52 Team Pursuit	Bill Brown	Riverside C.C. (California)
53 Off the Ground	Joe Cipp	Bellport H.S. (New York)
54 Stance and Start	Kevin Cosgrove	Wisconsin
55 Power Tackle	Bill Doba	Washington State
56 3-Step Pursuit	Chuck Driesburgh	Pittsburgh
57 Hide-a-Bag	Tom Gadd	Bucknell
58 Missouri Pursuit	Skip Hall	Missouri
59 Inside	John Herrington	Harrison H.S. (Michigan)
60 Make 5, Lose 5	Nick Hyder	Valdosta H.S. (Georgia)
61 Tackling Circuit	Jack Leipheimer	Allegheny
62 Drive Pursuit	Kevin Lempa	Dartmouth
63 Sideline Pursuit	Frank Lenti	Mount Carmel H.S. (Illinois)
64 Team Pursuit	Denny Marcin	Illinois
65 Pass Pursuit	Larry Marmie	Arizona Cardinals (NFL)
66 Wheel	Charlie McBride	Nebraska
67 Zone	Pete McGinnis	Arkansas State
68 Cones	Chris Smeland	Utah State
69 Goal Line Tackling	Carl Torbush	North Carolina
70 Squeeze	Bill Young	Ohio State

51 Open Field

Coach: Will Bowman
College: University of Toledo
Head Coach: Gary Pinkel

Purpose: To execute a perfect form tackle from a predetermined side.

Procedure:

1. One line of offensive players aligns 10 yards from a line of defenders. Place two square bags in front of the defenders.

2. Place three cones 5 yards apart to form one boundary. A coach (ball) stands behind the middle cone. The sideline forms the other boundary.

3. The drill starts after the coach throws the ball to the offensive player who is moving forward.

4. The tackler stands in a two-point stance and moves forward over the bags to gain ground on the ball carrier. He executes a gather technique while making progress toward the ball carrier in a correct football position.

5. After being wrapped up on contact, the ball carrier may execute a spin move.

Key Points:

- There are three positions in open-field progression: (a) the ahead phase, which is designed to reduce the angle; (b) the even phase, in which the tackler dictates the direction the ball carrier can take; and (c) the behind phase, in which the tackler is first to secure and then strip the ball carrier.

- The tackler must keep the ball carrier inside and in front by executing the inside pursuit technique (press football) to prevent a cutback.

- The contact point for the tackler is the inside hip of the ball carrier.

- Just before contact, the tackler gets his hips across, keeps his eyes under the chin, and takes shortened strides, keeping his chest "inside" his feet.

Open Field **51**

- Teach the tackler to grab the cloth so the ball carrier cannot hit and spin.
- If the tackler is not executing the gather technique, the coach should stop the drill.
- As the drill is repeated, the ball carrier can cut back to make sure the tackler is working inside out.

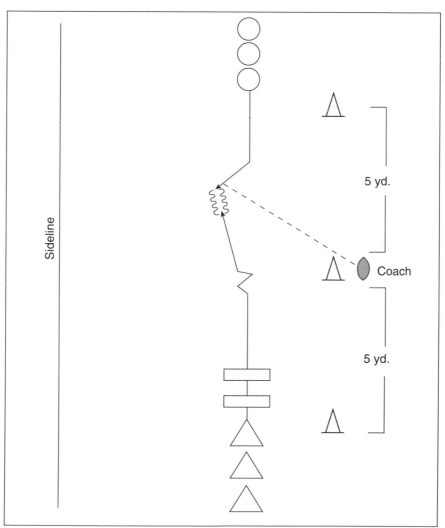

52   Team Pursuit

Coach: Bill Brown
College: Riverside Community College (California)
Head Coach: Barry Meier

Purpose: To execute proper pursuit angles to the football with team intensity.

Procedure:

1. Two coaches, B and C, align on the line of scrimmage just inside the sidelines. Another coach, A, aligns in the middle on the line of scrimmage. Another coach, D, calls signals behind the defense.

2. The team huddles in front of the middle coach. The defensive coach, D, calls a defense, and the team breaks the huddle and lines up in proper alignment.

3. The middle coach starts the drill by taking a snap. He simulates throwing the ball to either sideline coach.

4. The sideline coach fakes catching the ball and runs straight down the field just inside the sideline to score.

5. On the snap, the team does a down-up. The team then sprints at an angle to the sideline to which the simulated throw is directed.

6. While in pursuit, each defender works to cross the face of the ball carrier without impeding him.

Key Points:

- To avoid wasting time chasing bad throws or drops, simulate the throw and catch.

- Coach defenders to run full speed. During pursuit, they must be able to adjust their angles to cross the ball carrier's face.

- The defender must not trail the ball carrier from behind.

- To correct pursuit angles, the coach (D) calling signals positions himself downfield.

Team Pursuit

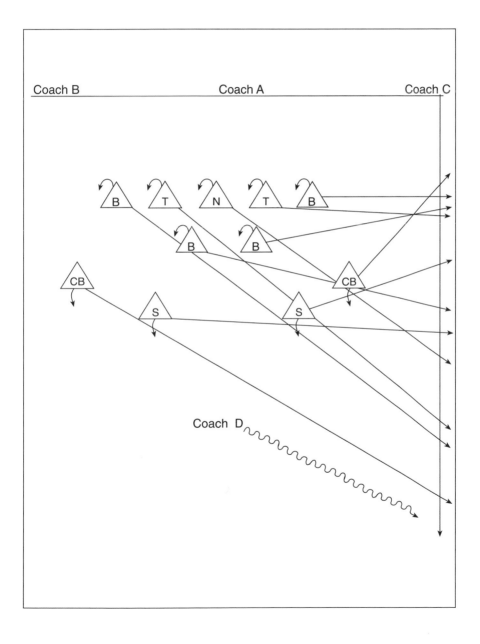

53   Off the Ground

Coach: Joseph Cipp
College: Bellport High School (New York)
Head Coach: Joseph Cipp

Purpose: To train defensive players to get off the ground and to find the football.

Procedure:

1. Three lines of players face the coach. To begin the drill, the first player in each line aligns in a four-point stance.
2. On the coach's command, each player dives out to his stomach, rolls to the right, does a somersault, and gets on his feet in a running attack position.
3. The player locates the coach and sprints through him.
4. The coach is continually backing up to accommodate the different agility drills.

Key Points:

- This drill puts a player on the ground in all the positions he might experience in a game.
- Train players to get off the ground quickly after their somersaults.
- The coach encourages players to sprint through him at full speed.
- After all players complete the drill, they go to the back of the line and repeat the drill by rolling left.
- While waiting their turns, the players are required to dress up their line.

Off the Ground 53

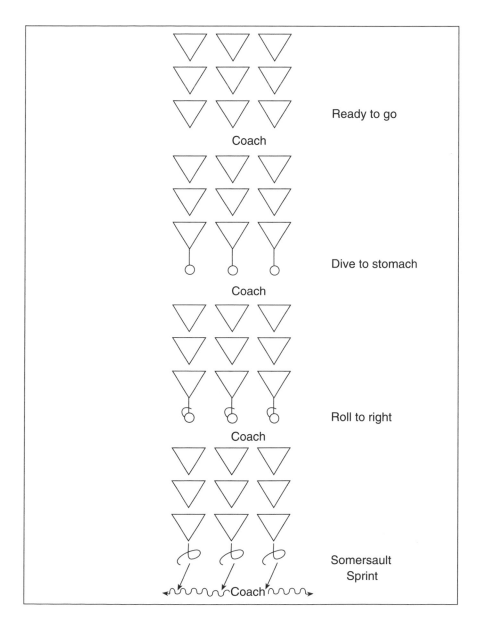

Ready to go

Coach

Dive to stomach

Coach

Roll to right

Coach

Somersault
Sprint

Coach

54 Stance and Start

Coach: Kevin Cosgrove
College: University of Wisconsin
Head Coach: Barry Alvarez

Purpose: To teach players how to maintain a correct football stance. To teach players a quick lateral shuffling movement and the ability to start, stop, and change direction quickly.

Procedure:

1. Align players on a yard line. If crowded, players may line up on a second line, offset so they can see the coach.

2. The coach positions himself in front of all players so that they can see him.

3. To start the drill, players stand erect with toes touching the line.

   a) On the command "breakdown," the players quickly assume a good football position, which they maintain for one minute.

   b) On the command "relax," they stand up.

   c) Repeat this portion of the drill three times. Each time, take 15 seconds off the clock.

4. During the second part of the drill, add a quick lateral shuffling movement. On the breakdown command the players align in a good football stance.

   a) The coach signals to the right or left with his arm. He directs the players to shuffle for three quick steps before stopping.

   b) Players shuffle to the right or left four or five times before the coach gives the relax command.

5. The third part of the drill starts with the quick lateral shuffling movement. Instead of letting the player stop after each movement, the coach must change his direction or movement.

Stance and Start 54

Key Points:

- Throughout the drill, players should keep a good football position; the coach reminds the players to stay on the line, not raising or lowering their bodies.

- Teach players to clear their cleats when shuffling. Do not allow them to use crossover steps.

- The coach checks for balance and lean after the players complete the three-quick-step shuffle.

- Coach players not to pause or lean while changing directions.

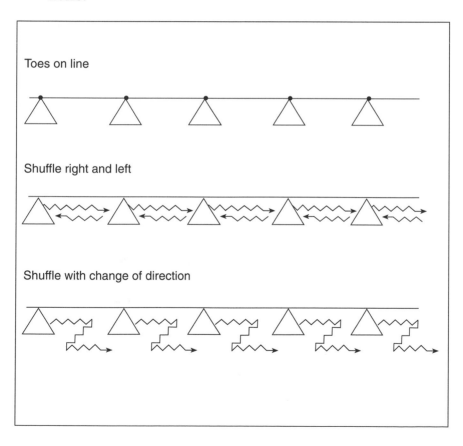

Toes on line

Shuffle right and left

Shuffle with change of direction

55 Power Tackle

Coach: Bill Doba
College: Washington State University
Head Coach: Mike Price

Purpose: To teach defensive players to wrap up, grab cloth, and hang on until the ball carrier is on the ground.

Procedure:

1. The ball carrier stands facing the sideline.
2. The tackler aligns two feet away in a good football position, head up and knees bent.
3. On command, the ball carrier turns and attacks the tackler.
4. After contact is made, anything goes as the ball carrier retreats, spins, or runs over the tackler.
5. The tackler attacks the ball carrier, wraps, and works to drive him back and take him to the ground.

Key Points:

- Unless the tackler wraps up and keeps his head up, he will lose the ball carrier.
- End the drill only when the tackler has put the ball carrier on the ground, not before.
- Until tacklers learn to wrap up and finish, they will miss many tackles. Be prepared for many missed tackles at first.
- This drill is a safe way to teach live tackling without a big collision taking place. This includes any mismatch that pits big against small.
- The more excited the coach gets, the more competitive the drill.

Power Tackle

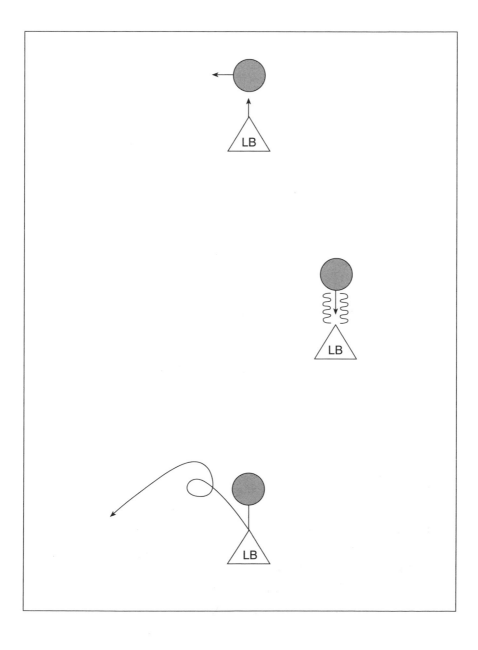

56 3-Step Pursuit

Coach: Chuck Driesbach
College: University of Pittsburgh
Head Coach: John Majors

Purpose: To teach defenders how to recognize formations, to run correct pursuit angles to the football, and to react correctly to the three-step pass.

Procedure:

1. The players align in a defense that is used against the three-step passing game.
2. Using different formations, the coach (QB) sets up a skeleton offense.
3. The QB sounds cadence. On the snap count, the QB executes a three-step drop and throws a hitch route to any WR. The RBs throw bags at the lower bodies of the DEs.
4. The defense reads and reacts to the QB's three-step drop. The defensive linemen work on a quick pass rush, moving while the DBs shuffle step.
5. All 11 defenders take a proper pursuit angle to the thrown ball.
6. The drill starts at the left hash before moving to the middle and to the right hash.

Key Points:

- Use cadence to develop defensive line discipline (key football).
- The defensive linemen must get their hands up to tip the ball or to obstruct the QB's throw.
- The RBs throw bags at the penetrating DEs to teach them to use their hands to defeat low cut blocks.
- While taking two to three short shuffle steps, the DBs read the QB's shoulders and nonthrowing hand.
- Insist that players align in the proper defensive call.
- The drill is over when all defenders end up at the ball.

3-Step Pursuit

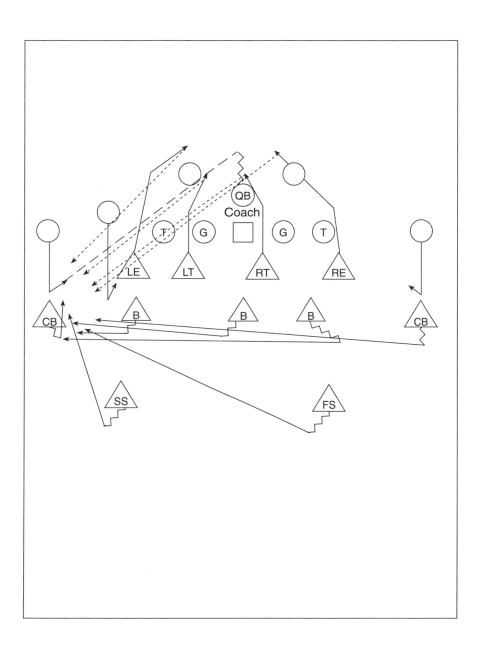

57 Hide-a-Bag

Coach: Tom Gadd
College: Bucknell University
Head Coach: Tom Gadd

Purpose: To develop a defensive attitude of all-out pursuit and to build team unity.

Procedure:

1. Divide the defense into three competitive groups.
2. One player from each group aligns on a line facing the drill coach.
3. Position two coaches, each holding a stand-up dummy, behind the three players.
4. On the drill coach's command, the three defenders do a series of seat rolls, crab moves, and so forth. The coach then gives the command "up," which brings the players to a standing two-point reaction position.
5. Immediately, the coach says "go," and the three defenders turn and find one of the two bags held by the coaches.
6. The three defenders run full speed to tackle two bags.
7. Penalize the defender who missed getting a bag by having him and his group do 5 to 10 push-ups or up-downs.

Key Points:

- Throughout the drill, the coaches holding the bags keep moving. They must stay away from each other.
- The most important part of the drill is the reaction of the other group members. The winners' groups run out, celebrate, and congratulate their players.
- If players are not excited or sincere in their celebration, penalize their group by having them do push-ups or up-downs.
- The drill lasts 5 to 10 minutes, which is enough time to establish habits of full-speed pursuit, being competitive, and having fun.

Hide-a-Bag

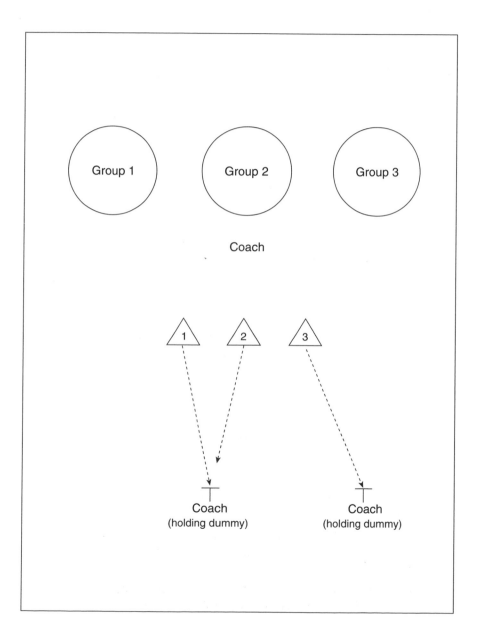

58   Missouri Pursuit

Coach: Skip Hall
College: Missouri
Head Coach: Larry Smith

Purpose: To develop and teach proper pursuit angles.

Procedure:

1. After the defense is called, players break the huddle and align in a defense.

2. Two RBs align with a coach (QB) against the defense.

3. On the snap, the QB pitches to either RB who then runs wide outside the cones and down the sideline.

4. After the snap, all defensive players take proper pursuit angles on the RB and attempt to two-hand tag him below the waist.

5. Each defender stops at the point of touch and chops his feet until the last defender has touched the RB.

6. When the last defender tags the RB, the coach blows his whistle. All defensive players hit their stomachs, bounce up, run off the field, sprint back to the ball, and get into a huddle.

Key Points:

- Each sideline coach looks to see that the RB is touched below the waist with two hands by every defender.

- Watch defenders. Make sure each runs a correct pursuit angle.

- Both feet of each defender must be out of bounds before he can sprint back to the ball.

- Station coaches to observe everything. Each coach gives a thumbs up or thumbs down to signify proper or improper technique.

- If a coach signals thumbs down, the same defensive squad runs the drill until they earn all thumbs up.

Missouri Pursuit

58

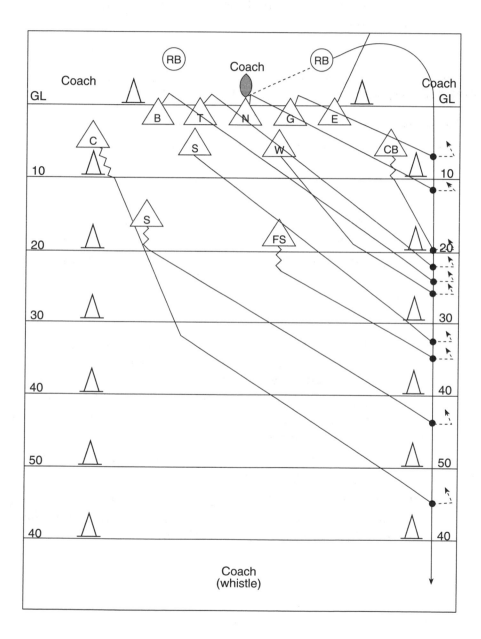

59   Inside

Coach: John Herrington
College: Harrison High School (Michigan)
Head Coach: John Herrington

Purpose: To drill the defense in ways to stop inside plays and to correct weaknesses in the defensive scheme.

Procedure:

1. Place two dummies as boundary markers just outside each DE (OLB).
2. The offensive scout team huddles to receive the play assignment.
3. To implement the defensive scheme, the defensive front seven aligns in a correct position.
4. Using a script of 10 to 12 plays, the scout team runs an inside running play on the snap.
5. Conduct the drill live with a quick whistle.

Key Points:

- The coach's script features the best inside running plays of the current opponent. Scripting 10 to 12 plays allows coaches to correct any defensive weaknesses that show.
- Examples of the scout coach's flip cards are as follows: (1) blast right, (2) off-tackle left, (3) buck trap, (4) dive, (5) slant trap, and so forth.
- Scout team running backs must run inside the dummies.
- The coach rewards the hardest hit. Then the players gather around to cheer and show enthusiasm.
- Occasionally, the coaches intentionally set up a weaker defense to see if it can still stop the play.

Inside **59**

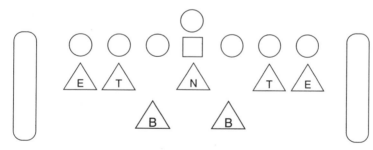

Scout coach

Defensive coaches

60　　Make 5, Lose 5

Coach: Nick Hyder
College: Former head coach,
　　　　　　Valdosta High School (Georgia)

Purpose: To teach team defense and field position awareness under game situations by going against a simulation of the opponent's offense.

Procedure:

1. Place the ball on the one-inch line. The offensive scout team is ready to execute coming out of the end zone.

2. At the line of scrimmage, the defensive team prepares to stop the scout team.

3. If the defense stops the scout team from gaining five yards, place the ball back on the one-inch line. If the scout team gains five or more yards, the next play starts at the point of the gain. Once the offense is beyond the five, for each down the defense wins, the offense loses five yards.

4. Assess all penalties during the scrimmage.

5. At the 50-yard line, the teams reverse direction. Now the defense works to stop the scout team from scoring.

Key Points:

- Field position dictates which defensive calls are made.
- At some point, the coach stops the drill, especially if the scout offense is struggling to move the ball.
- This drill promotes team unity, a possession attitude, and a controlled confidence.

Make 5, Lose 5

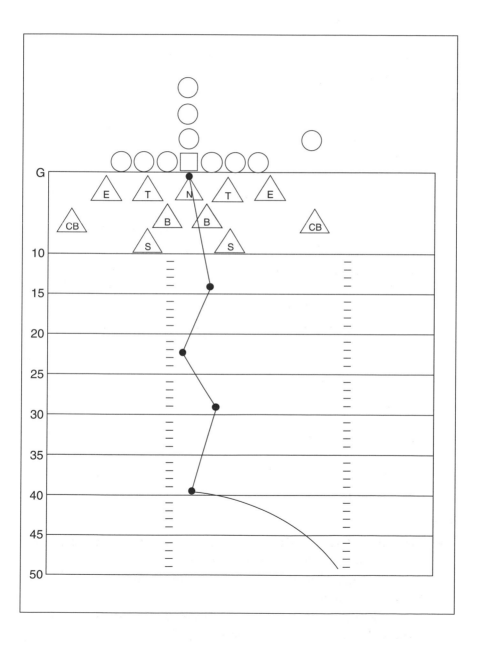

61   Tackling Circuit

Coach: Jack Leipheimer
College: Allegheny College
Head Coach: Ken O'Keefe

Purpose: To set the tempo for practice and teach proper tackling techniques.

Procedure:

1. Locate four tackling stations 20 yards apart:
   a) In the sideline and goal line corner is the mat drill: The defender, keeping square, lifts the ball carrier and drives him back on the mat.
   b) In the middle within the goal line area set up the eye opener: On command, the ball carrier chooses a hole to run through while the defender shuffles square, keeping tackling leverage on the ball carrier.
   c) In the middle of the field at the 20-yard line run the low block drill: The defender sheds a low block to attack and tackle the ball carrier upfield
   d) On the sideline at the 20-yard line work the score drill: The ball carrier runs on either side of a dummy; the defender reacts to attack and tackle the ball carrier before he crosses the sideline.

2. Each position coach takes his players to one of the designated tackling stations. The coach remains at his original station while the players rotate.

3. At each station, players execute specific tackling skills for two minutes. They have 30 seconds to change stations.

4. The specific drills can vary from week to week.

Key Points:

- Position players (DBs, LBs, DEs, DL) stay together to ensure best physical matchups.
- The position coach at each station teaches a specific tackling technique.
- The tackling circuit allows each defensive position coach to have personal contact with every defensive player daily.

Tackling Circuit

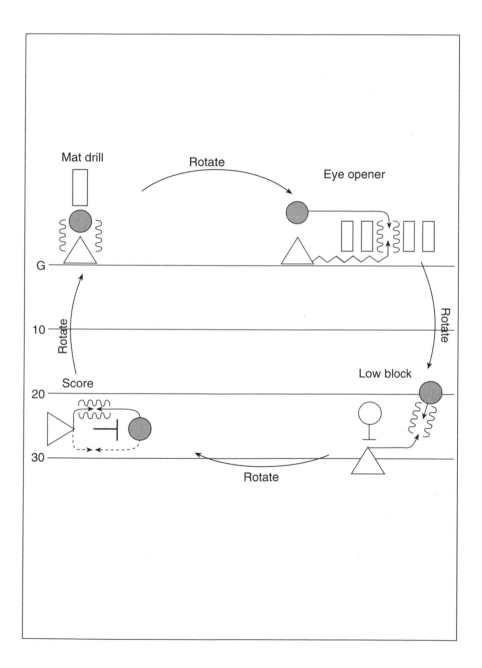

Mat drill

Rotate

Eye opener

G

Rotate

10

Rotate

Low block

Score

20

30

Rotate

62   Drive Pursuit

Coach: Kevin Lempa
College: Dartmouth College
Head Coach: John Lyons

Purpose: To prepare team defense by breaking huddle, executing proper alignment calls, and simulating game conditions when running to the football.

Procedure:

1. The defensive team huddles at the line of scrimmage, breaks the huddle, and aligns in the called defense.
2. The drill starts when the opposing QB (coach) simulates the snap.
3. The QB stands and points to one of five coaches who are spread all over the field.
4. The defense turns and runs in correct pursuit angles toward the designated coach.
5. Players circle around the coach, running in place, until the coach signals a break.
6. To simulate an offensive drive, repeat this drill five to eight times.

Key Points:

- The front seven can stem. The secondary can disguise coverage before the snap.
- Before the snap, all players should be in a good football stance.
- Place emphasis on having a good huddle and break.
- Players in pursuit must sprint. They must not follow the same-colored jersey.
- There is little risk of injury in this drill.

Drive Pursuit

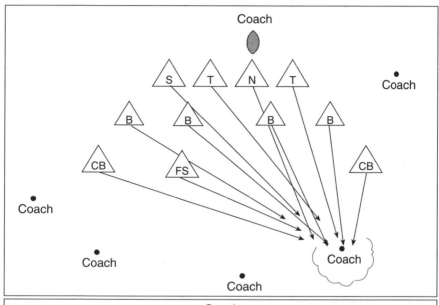

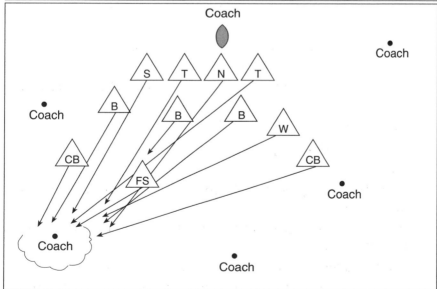

63   Sideline Pursuit

Coach: Frank Lenti
College: Mount Carmel High School (Illinois)
Head Coach: Frank Lenti

Purpose: To teach the defensive team proper pursuit angles to the football.

Procedure:

1. Place 10 cones 5 yards apart, 3 yards from each sideline.
2. The coach (ball) aligns on a yard line in the middle of the field.
3. Two lines of receivers and backs align 10 yards on each side of the coach.
4. The defensive team breaks huddle to align in the called defense.
5. On the snap, the team executes the first three steps of the technique versus air. The coach throws the ball to the first receiver or back in line.
6. The receiver or back sprints down the sideline. He must stay between the cones and the sideline.
7. Defenders locate the football and, taking a proper pursuit angle, sprint to the ball.
8. When pursuing, each defender stops at his designated cone.

Key Points:

- Teach defenders to run where the ball is going, not where it is.
- When the play goes away from the backside DE, he checks for the reverse.
- The ball must cross the line of scrimmage before the defender pursues.
- Teach players not to follow the same-colored jersey.
- Stopping at the designated cone prevents the defender from running past.

Sideline Pursuit

- Defenders must not impede the ball carrier from running the length of the cones.

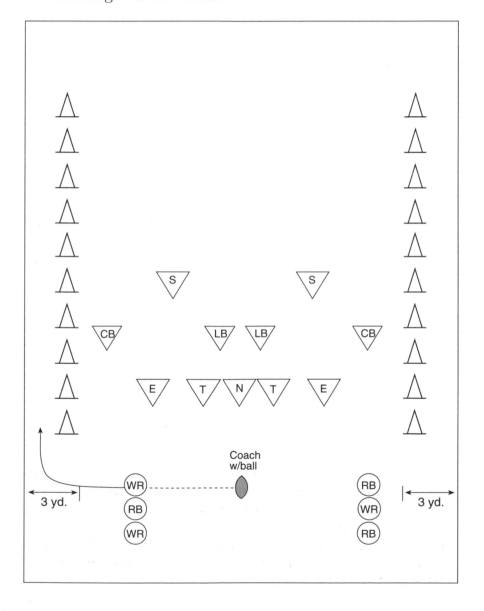

64   Team Pursuit

Coach: Denny Marcin
College: University of Illinois
Head Coach: Lou Tepper

Purpose: To teach defenders to pursue at the correct angle by sprinting to the ball whether it's a run or pass.

Procedure:

1. Place an alignment strip at the 20-yard line hash mark. Mark the strip with five offensive positions.
2. Place cones to represent the TE, FL, and SE according to formation. Managers play the two running backs.
3. Position two coaches on the sidelines and another coach in the middle of the end zone.
4. The defense aligns in the back of the end zone. On command, players sprint to form a huddle facing the end zone.
5. With the defensive call, the players break the huddle and align correctly on the strip.
6. On the snap, the QB tosses or throws the football to the manager.
7. The defense reacts to the run or pass by sprinting on correct pursuit angles. If it is a run, the players must find and circle the sideline coach in the direction of the run. If it is a pass, the front four rush the QB while the others play the coverage called. After a pass is intercepted, the entire defense runs through the goal line.

Key Points:

- Coaches correct every phase of the drill. The position coaches signal a thumbs-up if OK and call out the second unit. If a coach signals thumbs-down, repeat the drill with the same defense.
- During the pass rush, the front four allow the QB to throw the ball. Teach the pass defenders to intercept the thrown ball at the highest point.

Team Pursuit

64

- RBs do not run downfield. Too often the RBs never get where they are going because some defenders hold them up.

- Run the drill for four minutes once a week during the season.

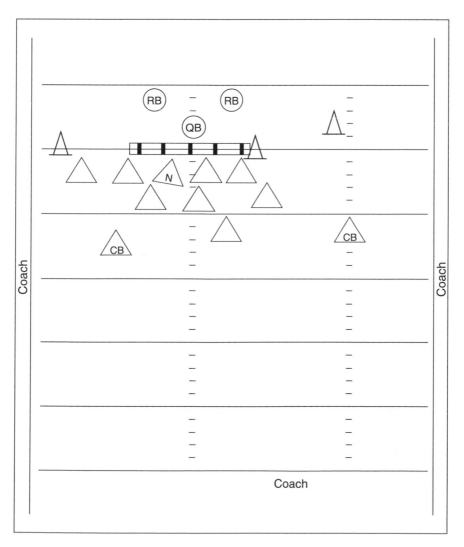

65 **Pass Pursuit**

Coach: Larry Marmie
College: Arizona Cardinals (NFL)
Head Coach: Vince Tobin

Purpose: To teach defenders the proper pursuit angle to the football after a pass has been thrown.

Procedure:

1. The defensive team aligns on the ball in the called defense.

2. The QB is the only player on the offensive side of the ball.

3. When the QB drops back to throw, the defensive line rushes the passer, LBs drop into their zone assignments, and DBs cover their zones.

4. The QB throws to any one of the DBs, who catches the ball (interception).

5. After the QB has thrown the ball, all defenders break full speed to the ball.

6. Upon reaching the intercepted ball, the defenders break down on the DB and stay until the coach claps them off. They run off the field.

Key Points:

- To start the drill, all defenders align in the correct stance.
- When going back to pass, the QB may take a three-, five-, or seven-step drop.
- To teach correct pursuit angle, the DB stays put after his interception.
- Position coaches watch their players run proper pursuit angles to the ball.
- This is an excellent drill to start or finish a defensive practice.

Pass Pursuit

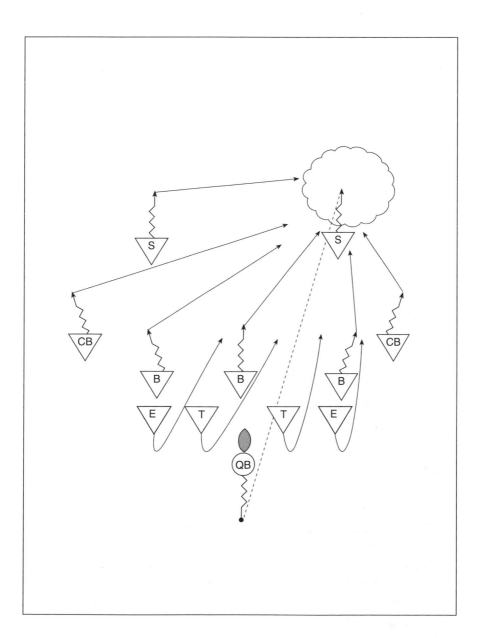

65

66 **Wheel**

Coach: Charlie McBride
College: University of Nebraska
Head Coach: Tom Osborne

Purpose: To teach players how to maintain body balance, develop foot quickness, and change direction quickly.

Procedure:
1. The defender aligns on his fingertips in a four-point stance with his hands in the middle of the four bags.
2. While in the starting position, the defender has his head up and his feet under his hips.
3. When ready, the defender starts by stepping over each bag in the circle, eventually returning to his original starting position.
4. When either foot hits the ground in the original starting position, the defender reverses direction, circling each bag one more time.
5. After returning to his original starting position, the defender explodes out of the four-point stance and runs over a bag two yards from the center.
6. The coach starts the timing procedure when the player's foot hits the ground after stepping over the first bag. He stops timing when the player's foot hits the ground after stepping over the final bag.

Key Points:
- Use five bags of any size.
- The defender's hands must stay and maintain contact with the center of each bag he crosses.
- While completing rotations, the defender keeps his knees up under his hips.
- The coach looks for quickness by the defender when he comes out of his four-point stance to run over the final bag.
- Timing each defender is an effective way to measure improvement.

Wheel

66

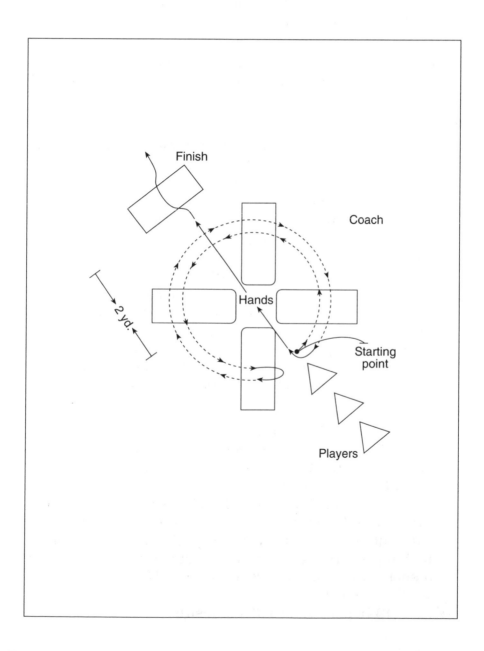

67   Zone

Coach: Pete McGinnis
College: Arkansas State University
Head Coach: John Bobo

Purpose: To teach defensive linemen and linebackers proper fit and reaction versus the inside and outside zone running game.

Procedure:

1. Three OL align on the line of scrimmage. The RB aligns seven yards deep, directly behind the middle blocker.
2. The defensive line aligns in a shade technique to either side of the middle blocker.
3. Two LBs align over the two outside blockers.
4. The coach stands behind the defenders, signals to the offensive line to block the inside or outside zone (right or left), and gives the snap count.
5. The coach calls cadence and the offensive line executes the play with defenders reacting to the blocking scheme.
6. The drill rotation has the outside blocker stepping out and being replaced while the other two blockers slide over. One LB slides over while the other one is being replaced. Use a different RB for each repetition.

Key Points:

- If a RB is used, he runs inside or outside of the zone depending on the blocking scheme. If the manager substitutes for the RB, he hand signals by pointing the flow and angle for the LB read.
- LBs work upfield to attack the blockers. Emphasize the proper fit between defensive line and backside LB.
- After all DL have rotated through the drill, use another technique to repeat the drill. Get maximum repetitions in a short time. Use OTs, OGs, OC, and TEs to simulate all blocking schemes.
- Add QB ballhandling skills if desired.

Zone

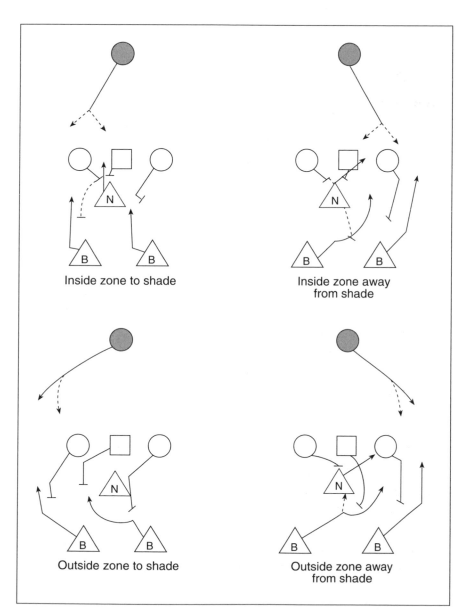

Inside zone to shade

Inside zone away from shade

Outside zone to shade

Outside zone away from shade

68 **Cones**

Coach: Chris Smeland
College: Utah State University
Head Coach: John L. Smith

Purpose: To teach defensive players the proper angle to attack the football.

Procedure:

1. Run the drill from the middle of the field. One coach aligns on each sideline-goal line corner, and one coach aligns in the middle on the goal line.

2. Starting at the three-yard line, place 11 cones three yards apart on each sideline.

3. After receiving the defensive call, all field defenders break the huddle and align in a correct stance.

4. The drill begins when the coach simulates a center snap and steps to his right or left.

5. On the snap, all field defensive players hit the ground, get back on their feet quickly, and immediately take the proper pursuit angle.

6. The defenders run toward one of the 11 cones.

7. As each cone is occupied, the defender must adjust his angle to occupy the next cone available. The cones are not assigned.

8. After the defenders occupy all 11 cones and face the goal line, the coach signals the defenders to sprint to him for a team break.

Key Points:

- To effectively learn pursuit, the defenders must run toward a cone.

- Throughout the drill, the coaches encourage all defenders to make an all-out effort. This results in a total team effort.

Cones

68

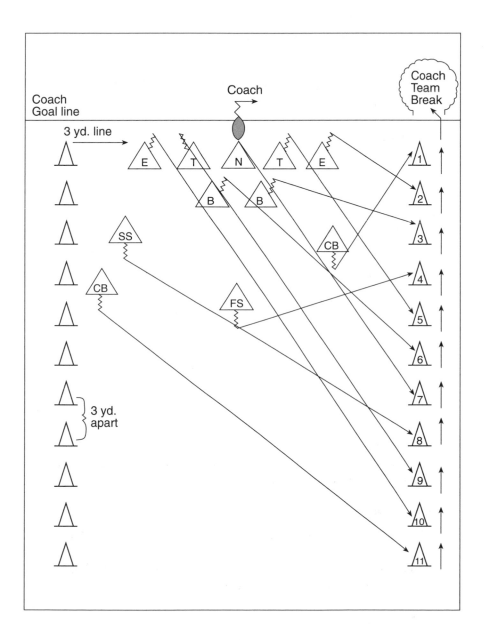

Coach
Goal line

Coach

Coach
Team
Break

3 yd. line

E   T   N   T   E

B   B

SS

CB

CB

FS

3 yd.
apart

1

2

3

4

5

6

7

8

9

10

11

69   Goal Line Tackling

Coach: Carl Torbush
College: University of North Carolina
Head Coach: Mack Brown

Purpose: To teach the tackling technique used in goal line and short-yardage situations.

Procedure:

1. Place the dummy one yard from the sideline (simulates the goal line) and directly in the middle of two five-yard stripes (simulates the sideline).

2. The tackler, in a hitting (LB) position, puts his heels on the simulated goal line while the ball carrier aligns one yard behind and directly in the middle of the dummy.

3. With the ball in his outside arm, the ball carrier assumes a broken-down position.

4. On the command "set," the tackler begins moving his feet and hands in a broken-down position.

5. The ball carrier counts "1,001 go" to himself before attempting to score by going close to the outside of the dummy, but not going out-of-bounds.

6. Upon the ball carrier's movement, the tackler works to get his helmet across the armpit of the ball carrier. Keeping his eyes on the football, he brings both arms forward in a double-uppercut movement while keeping his feet shoulder-width apart.

Key Points:

• The tackler keeps his feet active and shoulder-width apart to stop penetration. He maintains inside-out leverage to force the ball carrier out-of-bounds, preventing him from spinning inside to score and possibly creating a fumble by contact.

Goal Line Tackling 69

- The ball carrier stays inbounds and attempts to score by attacking, spinning back inside, and leveraging the tackler by being under his pads.
- Both ball carrier and tackler should keep their feet active.
- Because of the closeness of contact, this should be an injury-free drill.
- If there is a stalemate (no movement either way), or when the feet stop, stop the drill.

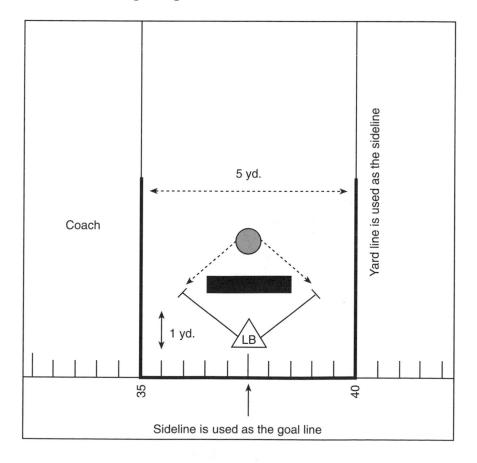

70 Squeeze

Coach: Bill Young
College: Ohio State University
Head Coach: John Cooper

Purpose: To teach the proper fundamentals and techniques used to defeat the base block (straight ahead).

Procedure:

1. Align three defensive linemen—one as an offensive blocker (OL), one as a running back (RB), and one as a defensive lineman (DL)—as diagrammed.
2. Place two cones (inside and outside) as diagrammed.
3. The OL aligns one and a half yards from the inside cone on the line of scrimmage. The RB aligns three yards deep between the inside cone and the inside foot of the OL. In a right shade, the DL aligns in a fundamentally correct three-point stance on the OL, in which his hand is behind the ball and his head is behind his hand.
4. On a predetermined or silent snap count, the OL fires off the line of scrimmage at half to three-quarters speed, base blocking the inside shoulder pad of the DL.
5. On movement of the OL, the DL extends out low from his stance, takes a power step with the inside foot, and stalemates the OL with a three-point contact: his outside hand is on the front cuff of the OL's outside shoulder, his eyes are at the top of the OL's outside numbers, and his inside hand is on the inside breast plate/armpit area.
6. On contact, the DL squeezes the OL's block to the inside and separates from the OL by extending his arms and locking out his elbows. Upon separation, he locates the RB, escapes, and tackles the RB.
7. On snap count or movement of the OL, the RB (ball) runs full speed between the OL and the inside cone. If the OL has been pushed into that area, the RB immediately cuts outside, running between the OL and the outside cone.
8. Upon contact, the RB pulls off, allowing the DL to make a fundamentally correct form tackle.

Squeeze

70

Key Point:

- If the ball is committed to the inside without threat that the RB will cut back into the gap, then the DL rips or swims across the face of the OL, throws the OL in the opposite direction, and tackles the RB.

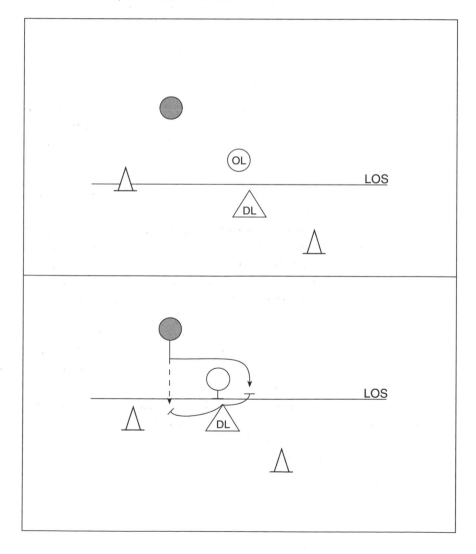

About the AFCA

Since its establishment in 1922, the American Football Coaches Association has striven to "provide a forum for the discussion and study of all matters pertaining to football and coaching" and to "maintain the highest possible standards in football and the coaching profession." These objectives, first declared by founders Alonzo Stagg, John Heisman, and others have been instrumental in the AFCA's becoming the effective and highly respected organization it is today.

The AFCA now has more than 8,000 members, including coaches from Canada, Europe, Australia, Japan, and Russia. Through three annual publications and several newsletters the Association keeps members informed of the most current rules changes and proposals, proper coaching methods, innovations in techniques, insights in coaching philosophy, and business conducted by the Board of Trustees and AFCA committees. A convention held each January gives members a special opportunity to exchange ideas and recognize outstanding achievement.

The Association promotes safety in the sport and sets forth strong ethical and moral codes that govern all aspects of football coaching. In addition, the AFCA is involved in numerous programs that ensure the integrity of the coaching profession and enhance the development of the game. It works closely with the National Collegiate Athletic Association, the National Association of Collegiate Directors of Athletics, the National Association of Intercollegiate Athletics, the National Football League, the National Football Foundation and Hall of Fame, Pop Warner, and other organizations involved in the game of football. Indeed, one of the many goals of the Association is to build a strong coalition—TEAM AFCA—of football coaches who will speak out with a unified voice on issues that affect the sport and profession.

The AFCA is the team of the football coaching profession. All current and former football coaches or administrators involved with football are encouraged to join. To become a member of the American Football Coaches Association, please write or call

American Football Coaches Association
5900 Old McGregor Road
Waco, TX 76712
817-776-5900

About the Editor

Dee Hawkes began his coaching career assisting former Stanford coach Jack Elway at Port Angeles High School in Washington. Over the next 29 years, he held four head coaching positions—at Department of Defense schools in Japan and Germany, at Davis High School in Yakima, Washington, and at Bothell High School in Bothell, Washington.

Hawkes has extensive experience as a football camp director and motivational speaker. Now a newspaper and magazine columnist, a book review editor, and an analyst for cable TV and radio, he remains committed to football.